READING THE SIGNS

Reading the Signs

A Sensible Approach to Revelation and Other Apocalyptic Writings

T. C. Smith

SMYTH & HELWYS
PUBLISHING, INC.
MACON, GEORGIA

ISBN 1-57312-156-8

Reading the Signs
A Sensible Approach to Revelation and Other Apocalyptic Writings

T. C. Smith

Smyth & Helwys Publishing, Inc.
6316 Peake Road
Macon, Georgia 31210-3960
1-800-747-3016

Library of Congress Cataloging-in-Publication

Smith, T. C. (Taylor Clarence), 1915–
     Reading the signs:
     a sensible approach to Revelation and other apocalyptic writings/
     T. C. Smith.
     p. cm.
     Includes bibliographical references.
     ISBN 1-57312-156-8   (alk. paper)
     1. Apocalyptic literature.
     2. Bible. N.T. Revelation—Criticism, interpretation, etc.
     I. Title.
     BS646.S65 1997
     220'.046—dc21   97-7919
                                                                                      CIP

Contents

Preface

My interest in apocalyptic writings goes back to my student days at Southern Baptist Theological Seminary, Louisville, Kentucky. In my New Testament introductory course it seems the professor did not have enough time left in the semester to give an interpretation of the book of Revelation. Later I discovered the real reason why he did not deal with the book. There was a verbal war being waged between premillennialists and postmillennialists in Christian circles. There were also amillennialists who considered the millennium as a matter of little significance. Thus, you were either a *post*, *pre*, or an *a*. I thought this was "much ado about nothing," but the controversy did whet my appetite to taste of the wares of apocalypticism, especially in the books of Revelation and Daniel where those engaged in the controversy centered their attention.

After completing my doctoral work at the seminary, I served as interim pastor of First Baptist Church, Roanoke, Virginia, for nearly a year. While in Roanoke, I encountered groups giving a detailed outline with charts of God's plan for the termination of the universe. Their interpretations were as wild, odd, fantastic, and preposterous as some of the mind-boggling and far-fetched dreams and visions of the apocalyptists. My appetite was whetted more to become engaged in a thorough study of Jewish apocalyptic literature. My exploration of this field of study was delayed, however. From Roanoke I went into the Naval Chaplain Corps during World War II. After being released from active duty at the end of the war, I enrolled in the graduate school of New College, University of Edinburgh, Scotland, to continue my theological pursuits.

When I enrolled at New College, I intended to write a dissertation on apocalyptic literature. Professor William Manson, my adviser, said that the range of literature was too immense and comprehensive for a dissertation unless the range of research was narrowed. His advice was sound and wise, but instead of limiting my scope of study, I chose another topic. In the meantime, Professor Norman Porteous, my

Syriac teacher, knowing of my interest in apocalyptic literature, suggested that I read H. H. Rowley's book *The Relevance of Apocalyptic*. The second edition of his book had just been published in July of 1947.

After reading Rowley's book, my interest in apocalyptic heightened. At the close of the final session at New College, I decided to go to Oxford University for the trinity term. On the way to Oxford, it was my good fortune to meet Professor Rowley at the University of Manchester. From that day until his death in 1968, he became my mentor in Old Testament and apocalyptic studies through correspondence and occasional visits in his home.

In March 1996, the occasion presented itself for me to renew my previous interest in apocalyptic literature when I was asked to deliver a lecture for the Dorsey and Maxine Horton Lectureship at Furman University. The title of the lecture was "The Future Was Then," and this book is an enlargement of that presentation.

I hope this book will serve as an appetizer for further study by those who are baffled by the symbolism of the writers of this sort of literature and act as a buffer against the cranks who make ill-founded predictions.

I gratefully acknowledge my indebtedness to my daughter-in-law, Diane, for typing my manuscript and to my wife, Ellen, who read the manuscript and made corrections.

Introduction

READING THE SIGNS

When I was five, my older sister made me shiver with fear and fright when she declared that the world was going to come to an end and would be consumed by fire. She gave me no reply when I asked her, "Why would God do this?" Then, in 1924, when I was nine, some charlatan from California set the time for the destruction of the world. His prediction made the front page of the local newspaper, *The Alexandria Town Talk*. He said the event was to occur at midnight on a particular date. The night of the foretold catastrophe arrived. I refused to go to bed that night at my regular time because I wished to witness the occurrence. I waited and waited and waited until three o'clock in the morning and could stay awake no longer. Through the intervening years I have not lost sleep over unwarranted predictions, but increasingly there has been an expanded interest in and an intensive study of apocalyptic works from which the prognosticators derive their systems.

As the year 2000 approaches, we are hearing all sorts of claims about Christ's appearing in the future and the termination of the age. Of course, this trend began some forty years ago when apocalyptic-minded individuals wrote books predicting the imminence of the battle of Armageddon. Apparently, there are many who cater to these forecasts of the future, since the sales for the books have skyrocketed. In addition to books foretelling the end time, we observe signs on bumpers saying such things as, "Jesus is coming soon," "In the event of the rapture, this car will be unoccupied," or "Maranatha." A number of ministers are caught up in this apocalyptic fever and preach on topics related to the last days. If you check the religion section of the Saturday newspaper, you will be amazed at the number of sermon subjects stressing the termination of the world. Since this is the temperament now, what will it be like in a few years as we get nearer to the next millennium? The bench mark for many prognosticators of the catastrophic intervention of God in human history hinges around the end of 1,000 years and the beginning of the next 1,000 years.

Instances can be cited from every century since the first century A.D. to the present day of mistaken predictors of the imminent end of the age. Montanus in the second century foretold the immediate advent of Christ, the establishment of a millennial kingdom, and the arrival of the New Jerusalem from heaven in Pepuza, Phrygia. From the time of Montanus until now, we have had ongoing predictions on the basis of "signs of the times" and "allegorical arithmetic" that the end was near. The contributors to this scheme of history were—to name a few—Tertullian, Jerome, Cyprian, Gregory the Great, Bernard of Cluny, the Joachites, the Millerites, the Darbyites, the Irvingites, the British Israelites, the Jehovah's Witnesses and finally modern fundamentalists and some conservative Christians. The chief sources for their calculations are the book of Daniel and the book of Revelation. Presumably, these forecasters had little or no knowledge of the basic tendencies of the type of literature represented by these two books. Furthermore, they show no acquaintance with the noncanonical Jewish writings of the same genre. Thus, they fail to understand apocalyptic fixed calculations that proclaimed the future was then. They accept as literal what the writers described in a symbolic fashion.

It is uncertain when and where apocalyptic literature received its label. Perhaps the name comes from the Greek word *apokalupsis* found in Revelation 1:1. The word means to uncover, reveal, or take the veil off. Since Revelation exhibited the characteristics of Daniel and noncanonical Jewish writings, the word apocalypse seemed appropriate for this literary type. This is a misnomer, however. Quite frequently the apocalyptists put on a veil rather than unveil, conceal rather than reveal, and close rather than disclose.

In times of crisis there is always an upsurge of interest in the apocalyptic, and confident predictions are made on the basis of its scheme of history. This is indeed true in the case of Daniel and Revelation. In the heyday of the Roman Catholic Church, the Pope was designated the beast in Revelation by those who were opposed to the Catholics. In the early part of the nineteenth century, there were those who said that Napoleon was the beast. During World War II, the interpretation was changed to Hitler. Following the death of Hitler, Stalin and his successors in the USSR became the incarnation of evil. With the collapse of the USSR, there has been no particular individual who can be pointed out as the personification of evil. As a result, apocalyptists make violent verbal attacks on groups. They oppose the World

Council of Churches, the Roman Catholics, Arabs, government, and any movement that is contrary to their own position.

The senselessness of apocalypticism of the last two centuries B.C. and the first century A.D. is quite evident on two counts. First, the erroneous predictions led to a lack of trust in the interpretations. Second, if a person studies the canonical writings of the apocalyptic vintage in relation to the noncanonical writings of the same ilk, he or she will observe that there are varieties of conceptions of the order of events marking the end of the age.

Concerning apocalyptic literature, even Daniel and Revelation, there is little to claim the attention of a majority of Christians. They know about Daniel who was thrown into the lion's den and the three friends of Daniel who were put into the fiery furnace, but the rest of the book is found less interesting and ignored. A few passages in Revelation are quite familiar, such as the letters to the seven churches in the Roman province of Asia Minor, or what is known from chapter 11 in Handel's "Hallelujah Chorus," but that is about all. On the other hand, there are those who elevate Daniel and Revelation to the highest level in the Bible and dedicate themselves to a minute study of them and, in so doing, neglect other portions of Scripture that have more permanent value. To them, these two documents have become the happy hunting ground to satisfy those who like to peer over the threshold of the yet to be.

When and why did apocalyptic literature originate? What are some of the characteristics of this sort of writing? What is the relationship of these works to prophetic oracles? What influence did they have on Judaism and Christianity? These and other questions enter our minds as we examine the teachings of these writers. But first, it is essential for us to consider the events, conditions, and circumstances in the history of Israel that gave rise to apocalypticism.

Chapter 1

THE SETTING
FOR APOCALYPTIC THOUGHT

When the Jews returned from Babylonian exile, they were assured of three things. These three elements gave a definite direction to the development of the political, religious, and social life of Judaism. The Jews were certain that Yahweh was the only God of the universe, that they were the elect of God, and that through God's providence they would achieve a glorious future. These hopes were firmly planted in their minds by Second Isaiah, the unknown prophet of the Exile whose oracles were incorporated in the scroll of historical Isaiah (chaps. 40–55).

Before the Exile, monotheism (the belief that only Yahweh is the God of the universe) may have been understood, but it was not plainly expressed. The eighth-century prophet Amos came very close to explicit monotheism when he pronounced God's judgment on the neighboring nations, but accurately stated Israel's religion from the time of Moses to the Exile was henotheistic (the belief of one God for a nation). The Hebrews worshiped one God, Yahweh, but they did not deny the existence of other gods. Moab had Chemosh, the Ammonites had Milcom, the Babylonians had Marduk, and the Persians had Ahura Mazda.

When the upper class of the Hebrew people was taken by Nebuchadnezzar as captives and transported to Babylonia, the change of a strange culture was a terrific shock to them. The Babylonians believed that their god Marduk was the creator of the world, the keeper of the tablets of fate, and the judge of all things to come. Their myth recorded in the *Enuma Elish* told of the fight between Tiamat and Marduk in which Marduk emerged the victor. In the midst of such claims, the exiles were pressed into the situation of reexamining their own faith in Yahweh. The two prophets of the Exile who gave assistance to their compatriots in captivity were Second Isaiah and Ezekiel.

Through his visions, Ezekiel consoled the people with the concept that Yahweh was present with them even if it was in a foreign land. He also assured the captives that they would return to their homeland, the temple would be rebuilt, and the kingdom of Israel would be resuscitated.

Second Isaiah went beyond the teachings of Ezekiel by affirming that Yahweh alone created the heavens and the earth (40:12) and "all the nations are as nothing before him" (40:17). There is no god except Yahweh (43:11; 44:6; 45:5; 45:18). Cyrus, the Persian king who conquered the Babylonians, though he did not know it, was anointed by Yahweh to free the Jews from captivity (45:1-5).

Second Isaiah sets before us true monotheism. Along with his upgrading Yahweh as the only God, this prophet also downgraded the idolatry of the Babylonians. He declared that their gods were handmade, weak, poor, and helpless (40:19; 44:14-17; 46:1ff.). In addition to proclaiming Yahweh as the God of the universe, the prophet of the Exile asserted that the Jews were to be missionaries to the Gentile world. They were to be "a light to the nations" (49:6) in order that God's salvation may extend to the end of the earth. According to Second Isaiah, the Gentiles were also a chosen people and were to participate in the glorious future with the Jews. Unfortunately, when the Jews were allowed to return to their homeland by the edict of Cyrus, instead of including the Gentiles as a part of their glorious future, they rejected them and became more narrow and exclusive in their religion, even more so than the prevailing view before the Exile.

The returning exiles under Zerubbabel and Joshua were at first so constricted by their view of the elect of God that they limited their religion to those who went into exile. The vast majority of the Jews who were not taken into captivity were excluded because there was the lurking suspicion that they had not remained true to Yahweh as they themselves had been. To make sure the Jews who remained in the land could not participate in their worship, they set up genealogies (Ezra 2:1-70; Neh 7:7-73; 1 Esdras 5:4-46 in the Apocrypha) as a proof of descent from the exiles before they could be accepted as the people of God. This original limitation could not be upheld, however, because, in the observance of the first Passover after the return (Ezra 6:19-22), the *am ha aretz* (the people of the land who had not gone into captivity) were permitted to participate in the observance of the Feast of Unleavened Bread that followed Passover. The permission was given provided the *am ha aretz* had separated themselves from the pollution of pagan worship. While not much of a concession by the rigorous

Jews, it shows us that some in their ranks were less stringent and pressed for a laxity in the rule.

During this early period of the restoration of Israel, another prophet who was a contemporary of Haggai and Zechariah appeared on the scene. His oracles were inserted in the scroll of the historical Isaiah (chaps. 56–66). He, like Second Isaiah, believed that the Jews should include the Gentiles in their missionary endeavors. The oracle of Isaiah 56:1-8 is a passage of considerable interest and importance for the history of the Jewish attitude toward the foreigners and the acceptance of converts.

The prophet took seriously the message of Second Isaiah that spoke of the Jews as "a light to the nations." He went out of his way to remove the restrictions imposed by Deuteronomy 23:1-7. The eunuch who was excluded from the congregation of Israel was promised as his reward of faith a remembrance far greater than progeny. The foreigner who joined himself to Yahweh was assured that he would be received. If he kept the Sabbath and held fast to the covenant, nothing could prevent him from entering the assembly of Israel. The prophet did not propose circumcision as an initiatory rite, but this is probably implied from the foreigner's obligation to keep the covenant. This oracle is a clear indication of a slackness in the more rigid rule of some Jews.

When Nehemiah returned to Jerusalem about the middle of the fifth century B.C. to build the wall, he was horrified by the laxity of the Jews mingling with the *am ha aretz* and aliens. The slackness did not come from the ordinary Jews but from the priests. Immediately he instituted a more stringent policy of separation (Neh 13:23-31). In 397 B.C., Ezra, commonly named the father of Judaism, returned to Palestine in the company of another wave of exiles. Ezra's policy was based on the belief that the new commonwealth should include only those Jews who had been in exile. The Jews who remained in Judah, the Samaritans, and the foreigners who had moved into the land from 586 to 397 B.C. were excluded by him. Ezra set forth a *habdalah* (separatist) movement that inaugurated a new era in Jewish religion. Exclusiveness highlighted by strict endogamy (marriage of Jews to

Jews), Sabbath regulations, and genealogies extinguished the Jewish light to the Gentiles and suppressed all missionary desire.

In spite of Ezra's separatist policy, some Jews did not submit to his views but retained a missionary zeal. This reaction was reflected in two anti-separatist writings of the Old Testament. (1) The book of Jonah shows that Israel had a duty to proclaim God's revelation to the pagan world, and that a separatist program was contrary to God's will. (2) The book of Ruth stood not only in opposition to Ezra's restriction on mixed marriages (Ezra 9:1-15), but also against the exclusion of the Ammonite and the Moabite from the congregation of Yahweh, which was advocated by Nehemiah 13:1-13 and Deuteronomy 23:3-6. Excluding the Moabite would mean that Ruth was not a part of Israel. The same would hold for David who was a descendant of Ruth.

When the exiles returned from Babylonia, they looked forward with eager anticipation to a period of prosperity and peace. The edict of Cyrus that gave them permission to return home probably fostered great outbursts of loud shouts, "Free at last, thank God, we are free at last." But this euphoria was short-lived when they faced the reality of still being under Persian domination. Where was the glorious age that Second Isaiah foresaw? "Have we not suffered enough for our sins by our stay in Babylonia?" Where were the dreams of Israel's national status? How could they be a world power when they were under Persian domination? Darius I, the Persian king who succeeded Cambyses in 522 B.C., established an administrative system in his empire that was foolproof against the revolt of any nation striving for independence.

Joshua, the high priest, and Zerubbabel, a descendant of David, who jointly were the official leaders of the Jews, were exhorted by the prophets Haggai and Zechariah to begin the reconstruction of the temple and urged the priests to purify the cultic worship. They were practical enough to perceive that the two projects were essential for the unification of the religious life of the community, but they had something far more important in mind. The unification of the religious life was a prelude for undertaking a revolt against the Persians and declaring independence after making Zerubbabel the messianic king on the throne of David. Apparently, the revolt was accomplished, but Zerubbabel was removed as governor of Judea by Darius and possibly executed.

Except for the reforms of Nehemiah in 444 B.C., and of Ezra in 397 B.C., there is little knowledge of other events occurring in Judaism during the reign of the Persians. Only one incident claims our attention. During the reign of Artaxerxes III (Ochus 359–339 B.C.), the Phoenicians led a revolt against the Persians in 351 B.C. Simultaneously, there was a rebellion in Egypt. The Jews could not resist the temptation to throw in their lot with the insurrectionists. After five years, the uprising was quelled by Ochus, and the Jews suffered severely. The Persians destroyed the town of Jericho, and, according to Josephus, "the Persians formerly carried away many ten thousands of our people to Babylon."[1]

Philip II, king of Macedonia, envisioned a unified Greece that could not only stem the tide of any further attacks by the Persians, such as the expeditions of Darius I and Xerxes I, but could also dominate the known world. Through bribery and other methods he was able to form the Hellenic League. Before Philip could realize his dream, he was assassinated in 336 B.C. His son, Alexander, became the heir to his ambitions. After the Hellenic League chose him as commander in 334 B.C., Alexander crossed the Hellespont to engage the Persians in battle. He routed the Persian army at Grannicus and Issus and moved south to Egypt, where he was hailed as a deliverer of the Egyptians. In 331, he advanced to the east and sealed the doom of Darius III and the Persians at the battle of Gaugamela. His exploits did not end with a decisive victory over the Persians but carried him farther eastward to the Indus River. When he died of fever in Babylon in 323, his realm extended from Greece to northern India.

History does not measure the greatness of Alexander in terms of the vast amount of territory he won. His greatest achievement was bringing the East and West together through the propagation of Greek culture. The Hellenic spirit of individual liberty, emancipation from tyranny of custom and tradition, the free exercise of scientific and critical inquiry, a love for the beautiful in art and literature, and the development of the body and the mind extended to all parts of the world under his policy of Hellenization. From the babel of the Greek dialects there sprang a Greek language intelligible to all Greeks and usable by all conquered people.

Alexander broke down racial and national barriers by encouraging his soldiers to marry Asiatic women. His aim was to establish a mighty empire that disregarded differences between Greek and barbarian, setting people free for international relationships. As his army advanced, he established Greek colonies that became centers for Greek culture. The intermingling of the races initiated a spirit of cosmopolitanism, a syncretism of religions, and an interest in the individual. While Persian Zoroastrianism and Babylonian religious ideas had influenced Judaism in previous years, Alexander doubtless paved the way for the influx of these old concepts that were revived by the apocalyptists.

Upon the death of Alexander, the vast empire was divided among his generals. Ptolemy seized Egypt and later laid claim to Palestine. His seizure of this territory incurred the anger of Seleucus, another general of Alexander, who became the ruler of Syria after the battle of Ipsus in 301 B.C. For more than a century, the Seleucids of Syria and the Ptolemies of Egypt struggled for the possession of Palestine. The Jews were thus thrown into the middle of the conflict.

Antiochus the Great, a Seleucid king, after three attempts to gain possession of Palestine from the Ptolemies, finally defeated the Egyptian army at the battle of Panium in 198 B.C. and wrested the land from Ptolemy V. The reign of Antiochus was significant for Jewish history, not only because Palestine ceased to be under Ptolemaic domination, but also because his reign witnessed the entrance of Romans into Asiatic politics.

Because of Antiochus' unsuccessful armed opposition to the extension of Roman domination, Rome imposed heavy war indemnities upon Antiochus and his political territory. In addition to tribute, the Romans compelled him to furnish hostages for the payment of indemnities.

The attitude of the Jews toward Antiochus the Great was favorable at first. They were pleased to change their loyalty from the Ptolemies to the Seleucids, though there were Jews who dissented.

Antiochus favored the Jews by relieving their taxation burden. He even went so far as to exempt the temple personnel from taxation. When the Seleucid king was faced with huge war indemnities, however, he made heavy monetary demands, and the Jews felt betrayed.

Antiochus the Great was killed in the battle of Elam in 187 B.C., and his son, Seleucus IV (187–175), ascended the throne. As king, he followed an ill-advised policy in his treatment of the Jews. Seleucus sent his general Heliodorus to Jerusalem to seize the Temple treasure. A full account of this incident occurs in the apocryphal writing 2 Maccabees. Heliodorus was unsuccessful in this venture. In 175 B.C., Heliodorus had ambitions of becoming the ruler of the Syrian empire and killed Seleucus IV. His plans did not materialize, however, because Demetrius, the son of Seleucus IV, seized the throne.

Antiochus, the son of Antiochus the Great and brother of Seleucus IV, usurped the throne from Demetrius and ruled from 175 B.C. to 162 B.C. Antiochus conceived the idea of reviving the Olympian gods of Greece and used them as instruments of unity for the empire. He believed that the only way to maintain unification of the empire was through the establishment of one religion. Thus, he decided to make Zeus supreme again. Actually, the statues of Zeus he erected bore a striking resemblance to Antiochus. He became known as *Theos Epiphanes* (God Manifest) and demanded that he be counted among the gods. Halos found on his coins verify his claim of deification.

From the time of Alexander the Great until the accession of Antiochus Epiphanes, Hellenistic influence had gradually penetrated Palestine. The more liberal Jews did not see anything wrong with the acceptance of Greek culture so long as it did not impinge on the core of their religious beliefs. Yet, the more conservative Jews looked with disfavor on any innovations. The prevalence in Palestine of Greek worship and athletic festivals, coins bearing Greek inscriptions, emblems of Greek deities, and evidence for many towns bearing Hellenic names, all bear witness to the fact that Hellenistic culture and religion permeated the land of Palestine. If Antiochus Epiphanes had not resorted to violent means for the Hellenization of the Jews in

Palestine, it is likely they would have gradually submitted to Hellenism in a peaceful manner up to the limits of their acceptance.

The Syrian king was a man of violent impulses. When opposed he could become furious and cruel. His dream of overcoming the Romans and releasing the Syrians from huge war indemnities inherited from his father became an obsession with him. He believed that the only course of action available for him was to force the people throughout his domain to accept Greek culture.

The Jews were not entirely exempt from blame for the later severe action of Antiochus Epiphanes. From the time of the removal of Zerubbabel as governor of Judea by Darius I, the high priest had been the leader of the Jews in both religious and political affairs. When Antiochus Epiphanes seized the Syrian throne, Onias III was the high priest. Jason, the brother of Onias, bribed Antiochus and was appointed high priest. Onias was pro-Egyptian in his sympathies, while Jason was pro-Syrian. To Antiochus, the appointment of Jason was nothing more than making him a local governor. From the orthodox Jewish point of view, however, it was quite different. The orthodox Jews regarded the high priest as of divine appointment, and no human power had the right to interfere. Though Jason was of the high priestly family, this did not lessen their resentment.

If Jason could bribe the Syrian king and obtain the office of high priest, so could someone else. That someone else was Menelaus, who was not of the high priestly family. When Menelaus was involved in the murder of Onias and pressed his brother Lysimachus into stealing the holy vessels of the Temple, the orthodox Jews as well as the more liberal Jews turned against him. They waited for the opportune time to depose Menelaus. That opportunity came while Antiochus Epiphanes was leading an expedition against Egypt. Jason led an attack against Menelaus and captured the city of Jerusalem. Already halted by the Romans in his attempt to take Egypt, and angered by the embarrassment of having to submit to Roman authority, Antiochus returned to have his rage augmented by the revolt of Jason. He was in no mood to tolerate any dissension in his empire. If he had any hope of ever defeating the Romans, he must have absolute unity. He saw that the real problem with the Jews was their religious beliefs. Therefore, he concluded that he must embark on a forced policy of Hellenization that would be complete in all details.

Antiochus decided to make the Jews follow his own religion, which was the rebirth of the Olympian deities. In order to do this, he had to abolish the Jewish religion. He decreed that the daily sacrifice in the temple should be discontinued. An altar to Zeus Olympus was erected on the altar used by the Jews for burnt offering. Swine were offered as sacrifices in the temple, and copies of the Law were destroyed. The penalty for possessing a copy of the Law or practicing the rite of circumcision was death. He also declared that Sabbath observance was illegal. Most of these decrees came in the month of Kislev in 168 B.C. At first, there was only passive resistance by the Jews who refused to submit. When the persecutions of Epiphanes became more severe, however, active resistance became inevitable.

Leadership for the organization of active resistance came from the town of Modin near Lydda. There, an aged priest by the name of Mattathias, who was of the lineage of a certain Hasmon, refused to perform sacrifices to the pagan gods. A renegade Jew in the company of the king's officer stepped forward to offer the sacrifice, and Mattathias killed him on the altar. He then turned on the king's officer and killed him.

Mattathias knew that this was the time to act, so he summoned all the Jews who were zealous for the Law to follow him and his five sons in a guerrilla war against the Syrians. This revolt occurred in 167 B.C. When Mattathias died, the leadership of the movement fell to his son Judas. After several successful skirmishes against the Syrian forces, Judas took possession of Jerusalem. On the 25th of Kislev (December) in 165 or 164, he entered the temple and destroyed the altar that had been dedicated to Zeus. He also renewed the sacrifices to Yahweh. Afterwards, the day was observed as an annual festival and continues to be observed by the Jews as the Festival of Hanukkah.

With religious freedom once more restored in Jerusalem, many of the Chasidim (the pious ones) decided that this victory was sufficient. Judas was not willing to settle for anything less than political freedom, however. His pious followers, the Chasidim, were bitterly opposed to the ambitious designs of Judas and refused to continue to fight. In order to maintain a fighting force, Judas had to resort to the hiring of mercenaries. He continued his skirmishes against the central government until finally, in 160, with only 800 men left in his army, his career came to an end when he was killed in the battle of Elasa.

It was during this time of turmoil and suffering that the faithful Jews expressed an increased anxiety concerning the justice of God. Why would God allow a pagan ruler to do what he did? How could God tolerate the profanation of the Temple? Had God spurned the chosen people? Since God chose Israel of old, did God not remember the covenant with Israel? Why did not God get involved in Israel's shame?

Psalm 74 seems to have been composed during the period of the Hasmonean revolt, and the psalmist expressed the above cries of despair. This psalm and others were the soil out of which apocalyptic thought grew. It was in the midst of those chaotic times that the book of Daniel was written.

Note

[1]Josephus, quoting Hecataeus of Abdera, *Against Apion* I, 194.

Chapter 2

THE ORIGIN
OF APOCALYPTIC LITERATURE

It is a mistake to assume that Daniel was the first to delve into ideas that come under the rubric of the apocalyptic. To be sure, his was the first writing to portray most of the characteristics of later apocalyptists. The forerunners of this type of literature in Judaism were Ezekiel, the apocalyptic section in Isaiah (chaps. 24-27), the Isaiah of the Restoration, and Second Zechariah (chaps. 9–14).

The earlier chapters of Ezekiel that relate his visions symbolizing the majesty and power of God are the basis for the revelations received by the apocalyptists through angels, dreams, and visions. Ezekiel was influenced by the prophecy of Jeremiah concerning the invasion of a foe from the north (chaps. 3–6). In chapters 38–39, he revived the prophecy of Jeremiah and introduced a mystical king by the name of Gog who ruled over the land of Magog. In a cataclysmic battle against Gog, this Gog was defeated by God's intervention. The prediction of Ezekiel formed the basis for later apocalyptic works. In the Sibylline Oracles and in the book of Revelation, however, two figures appear. Rather than being Gog of the land of Magog, we discover Gog and Magog.

From Ezekiel's time forward, apocalyptic elements increased. An early apocalypse inserted into the scroll of the historical Isaiah (chaps. 24–27) introduces images of the end of times that were used by writers of other periods in history. The document is dated variously. Some scholars believe it was written in the third century B.C. during the rivalries of the Ptolemies and the Seleucids. Others place it around 200 B.C., which makes it close to the time when Daniel wrote. The apocalypse tells of the emptying and spilling out of the inhabitants of a world turned upside down (24:l), followed by the consuming of most people by fire (24:6), leaving the kings of the earth and the host of heaven to be cast into Sheol and punished (24:21).

In 26:19, we discover the first reference in the Old Testament to a resurrection from the dead. It is a resurrection of the righteous dead to life on earth. There is no indication of the resurrection of the apostate Jews or the wicked of other nations. Some scholars say that 26:19 is nothing other than a teaching of national resurrection similar to what we find in Ezekiel's vision of the valley of dry bones. Even if the prophet did not set forth individual resurrection, the passage played a significant role in preparing others for this concept. This section of the scroll of Isaiah by its phraseology indicates some acquaintance with Persian Zoroastrianism. Later we will present some of the Iranian teachings that crept into Judaism.

In the fifth century B.C., the prophet of the restoration (Isa 56–66) proclaimed a new heaven and a new earth (65:17; 66:22). Here, too, are traces of Iranian influence. Though it might just be that the prophet had nothing more in mind than a transformation of the present earth, the later apocalyptists were quick to use the re-creation of the universe motif and join with it the paradise or garden of Eden motif whether they borrowed from Zoroastrianism or from this prophet. In passing, we can refer to Revelation 21:1ff. where John introduces the idea in his apocalypse.

Joined to the work of Zechariah (chaps. 1–8) are two short collections of oracles we cannot ignore, though they are very difficult to interpret. The two collections (chaps. 9–11; 12–14) are not from the same hand, but it is impossible to identify the authors. Most assuredly they were not given by Zechariah. It is generally agreed that the two prophets delivered their oracles in the early Greek period of control over Palestine. The oracles are full of allusions to contemporary events and portray a pessimistic outlook, an otherworldly view, the use of symbolism, and other characteristics peculiar to apocalyptists. This literary style intended to depict contemporary events as well as the coming end had become a familiar way of thinking among the Jews so that when Daniel was written, the Jews were in a position to comprehend his message. Contrary to apocalyptic thought that gave no hope for the Gentiles in the coming age, these oracles show signs of grace for the non-Jews by including them under the realm of God. Of course, it is not a voluntary acceptance of God by the Gentiles. They are to be coerced by threats to worship God because the age to come demands it.

The first to make the journey into the bizarre and mind-boggling territory of apocalypticism was Daniel. Admittedly, there are those who contend that the date of two sections of the composite document of 1 Enoch precede Daniel. H. H. Rowley has furnished sufficient evidence to prove that the argument for the priority of 1 Enoch cannot be established.[1] We will pursue our study on the basis of his conclusions.

The book of Daniel was written about 168 B.C., during the time that Antiochus Epiphanes sought to abolish the Jewish religion with his forced policy of Hellenization. It purports to be written in the time of the Babylonian Exile, but the accumulation of evidence does not substantiate the claim.

Daniel is not listed among the prophets section in the Hebrew canon of the Old Testament, which was closed about 200 B.C. Rather, it was placed in the writings section of the Jewish tripartite division between Esther and Ezra-Nehemiah. There is no reference to Daniel in Ezra-Nehemiah and Chronicles, both of which were written after the Exile. Ezekiel 14:14, 20 clearly shows us that Daniel was not a contemporary person of the Exile but a figure of the past. The first allusion to Daniel is in the Sibylline Oracles III. 388-400, written in 140 B.C. First Maccabees, an apocryphal work written at the end of the reign of John Hyrcanus in 104 B.C., refers to Daniel who was put in a den of lions.

The author of Daniel took some legendary stories about a man named Daniel who was transported to Babylon with other Jews after the siege of Jerusalem by Nebuchadnezzar. After adapting the legends (found in chaps. 1–6) for his own purpose, he wrote anonymously. In chapters 7–12, which are apocalyptic visions, the anonymous author assumed the name of the hero about whom he wrote. The author of Daniel took the stories about Daniel and his three friends and extolled their piety and devotion to God so that he could use them as examples for Jews under the threat of death for their faith in his own day. After writing the stories of the past sprinkled with indirect suggestions here and there about Antiochus' relentless effort to blot out the Jewish religion, the author composed visions for the present situation of the Jews. He supported the Jews with comfort and hope in a time of suffering and despair. He assured his readers that God would intervene in history shortly and destroy their enemies.

Why did the author of the book of Daniel write under the guise of a Daniel? There was a Daniel known to us today from the Ras Shamra texts of the fourteenth century B.C., but that Daniel does not fit the description of our Daniel. Perhaps he wanted to show that a person living in jeopardy in Babylon during the time of the Exile could be used to give solace to a persecuted pious people in his own day.

Most all succeeding apocalyptists imitated the pattern laid out by Daniel, although the successors introduced more foreign material in their works and expanded on some of the message of Daniel. Yet we are safe in saying that Daniel was the forerunner in the field. Probably those who copied him were not satisfied with an insignificant Daniel as a pseudonym, so they latched onto the great worthies of the past. They wrote under the name of Adam, Enoch, Moses, the sons of Jacob, Baruch, Solomon, Abraham, and Ezra. The esoteric quality of later apocalyptists stems from the fiction of sealing the book of Daniel "until the time of the end" (Dan 12:9). The one writing under the guise of Daniel meant to give credence to the book filled with predictions of the imminent end of time. The imitators of Daniel attributed to the above saying a quality that was not essential, but it became a stock-in-trade among visionaries.

We might ask: Why did the apocalyptists write under a false name? The conventional answer is that by the time the prophets section of the Old Testament was closed, nothing else could be admitted, not even the book of Daniel. Yet, in 2 Maccabees 4:46, there was some question about what to do with the altar in the Temple that had been desecrated by Antiochus. The decision was made to tear it down and remove the stones to a convenient place until a prophet should come and tell them what to do. Thus it seems that the Chasidim (pious ones) still held fast to the value of prophetic oracles. Some thirty years later, the Pharisees rose to power and considered themselves to be the successors to the prophets. Since the apocalyptists wrote under the name of ancient authorities, perhaps they supported a revelation of the far distant past as having more value than the new revelation of the present.

Did the apocalyptists set out to intentionally deceive the people? Probably some of them did. Pseudonymity became artificial when it was slavishly and intensively copied by imitators. Remember, at that time the Jews had no real concern about who wrote any book in the Old Testament. The interest in authorship came from the rabbis of the fourth and fifth centuries A.D. when the two Talmuds were compiled.

Daniel in the Old Testament and Revelation in the New Testament are two canonical examples of a whole range of writings in a style that was tremendously popular in certain circles during the two centuries before Christ and that continued for more than 100 years thereafter. The two documents are representative of a vast amount of literature. Most of the writings are extinct; however, we have sufficient documents that are extant so that comparisons can be made with ideas existing in the canonical works. In the Apocalypse of Ezra, a book written shortly after the fall of Jerusalem in A.D. 70, the writer says that there were seventy books in addition to the twenty-four books representing the Old Testament (14:44-46). We assume that seventy books were apocalyptic because he said they were to be given to the wise among the people. "For in them is the spring of understanding, the fountain of wisdom, and the river of knowledge" (14:46-47).

Chief among the apocalyptic writings prior to the first century A.D. were canonical Daniel, the Testaments of the Twelve Patriarchs, Jubilees, 1 Enoch, and the Life of Adam and Eve. In the first century A.D., and possibly later, noncanonical writings were the Assumption of Moses, 2 Enoch, the Apocalypse of Ezra, the Apocalypse of Baruch, and the Sibylline Oracles. With the exception of Daniel, these documents do not appear in Hebrew or Aramaic. Christians took over the writings and translated them into Greek, Slavonic, Syriac, Latin, Ethiopic, Arabic, and Armenian. Admittedly, we do have fragments from fourteen manuscripts of Jubilees, fragments from 1 Enoch representing eleven manuscripts, and fragments of a few copies of the Testaments of the Twelve Patriarchs. All of these come from discoveries near the Qumran community.

Judging from the preponderant number of documents pieced together, the scroll on the *Wars of the Sons of Darkness and the Sons of*

Light, and certain of their hymns, the community of Qumran held to the apocalyptic ideas. Even before the discovery of the scrolls near Qumran, we knew something about the Essenes from the Jewish historian Josephus who wrote in the latter part of the first century A.D. Josephus had gone through two of the four stages of initiation into the Essenic community. There seems to be little doubt that the Essenes were the same as the community of Qumran. Josephus said that this dissenting group had divine revelations and believed that fate governed humankind, and that nothing happened to human beings that was not determined. He further said that the Essenes preserved books belonging to their sect. They named angels and foretold things to come by reading their holy books.

Apocalyptists Versus Prophets

How did the apocalyptists differ from the prophets of Israel? The prophets generally represented God's purpose in history, at least in part, as conditional on the people's conduct. Occasionally, they foretold the future, but they affirmed that the actual events were dependent on what the people did. Thus, the teaching of free will was one of the characteristics of their thought pattern. Both prophets and their successors, the Pharisees, were anxious to direct the will of the people in the direction of the will of God. The apocalyptists were determinists. They looked upon history as the working out of a predestined plan, and nothing could change that plan.

Note. The predictive element was not the forte of the prophets. Their predictions were not always fulfilled. In fact, Jeremiah found his nonfulfillment of predictions an embarrassment. He sharply accused God of letting him down (20:7ff.). The predictions of the prophets were unlike those of the apocalyptists. The prophets foretold the future that was to arise out of the present, whereas the apocalyptists foretold the future that would break with the present. When the prophets saw sin and wickedness, they understood what the harvest would bring. In a sense, they were ministers of doom, yet they did not speak only of doom. They could see with penetrating eyes through the darkness to a more distant future that gave glimpses of the glory the righteous remnant would inherit when evil had consumed itself.

The apocalyptists had a little faith in the present age to beget a better future. This is why they were called pessimists. They looked for a great intervention of God in history about to arrive in their own time. To the prophets, for the most part, the great empires of the world were merely instruments in God's hands to exercise God's will on the faithless people of Israel. The apocalyptists viewed the great world empires as adversaries of God who proudly resisted God's will. But they could not be successful; they would be annihilated. Certainly, we cannot make too sharp a distinction here because there are some apocalyptic elements contained in a few prophetic oracles, but these elements in the oracles are not dominant.

The prophets spoke from the standpoint of the present, whereas the apocalyptists retroceded into the past, assumed the name of some worthy person of the past recorded in the Scriptures, and wrote as though that person gave the revelation. They believed there was more validity for an ancient revelation than there was for the new. The apocalyptists, under the guise of prophecy, recorded events of former years to set the stage for the great unfolding denouement of history that was to be in their own time.

The prophets generally appealed to their listeners on the basis of reason and conscience, while the apocalyptists preyed upon the emotions and imaginations of the people. The apocalyptists received their revelation through intermediaries such as angels, visions, and dreams and emphasized the promises of God they discovered through their avid study of the Scriptures, especially the prophets. On the other hand, the prophets came to the people announcing, "Thus says Yahweh" or "The word of Yahweh came to me." Furthermore, they stressed the necessity for the people to obey the commandments of Yahweh. The demands of God were clarified even more by the rabbis, not only by the written law, but also by the oral law that was codified by Jehuda Ha-Nasi around 200 A.D., known as the Mishnah.

Note

[1]H. H. Rowley, *The Relevance of Apocalyptic* (2nd ed) (London: Lutterworth Press, 1947) 77-84.

Chapter 3

THE TEACHINGS
OF THE APOCALYPTISTS

Apocalyptic teachings cover a wide range of ideas, most of which are strange, weird, and fantastic. The visionaries were illogical, inconsistent, and incoherent in their messages. Over a period of 300 years, the vagaries of time induced alterations in a teaching of a previous writer. There is no agreement relative to their concept of the end of the age. Nevertheless, we must commend them for their loyalty and zeal for God in the time of despair and suffering.

The most significant and enduring contribution of the apocalyptists was their belief in the resurrection of the dead. For Christians, this precept is verified by the resurrection of Jesus, but for most Jews, it is a hope without any standard of reference. Previous to the Maccabean period, the religion of Israel made provisions for a continued existence after death in some sense, yet it was a survival not too appealing to the Jews. When Jews died, they went to Sheol, a subterranean abode similar to Hades among the Greeks. There they were confined, and the return to earth was impossible. The road to Sheol was a one-way trip, a place of silence, a land of no return. From the warm realities of life on earth a person moved to the cold semblance of a ghostly type of existence in the realm of the dead. Since this hope of an afterlife lacked vitality, the religion of Israel stressed the doctrine of survival through the family. It was social immortality, the continuance of life through descendants. Therefore, it was essential for the Jews to have children.

When the Jews began to recognize the importance of the individual apart from the corporate relation to Israel (teachings of Jeremiah and Ezekiel), and when they observed that retributive justice did not come in this life, their dynamic faith in a just God led them to the belief in the resurrection from the dead. There are only two explicit affirmations of this teaching in the Old Testament. One occurs in Isaiah 26:19, to which we have previously referred as a late insertion in the scroll of Isaiah. The other reference is in Daniel 12:2, penned by a man who had a deep and abiding faith in God during the Maccabean revolt.

Some scholars disregard the passage in Isaiah because of the way it speaks of national restoration, not individual resurrection. If we accept this interpretation and discard the verse as a reference to the resurrection of the individual, the only clear and undisputed passage in the Old Testament is Daniel 12:2. The author of Daniel faced the persecuting hand of Antiochus Epiphanes and believed that those who were loyal to God would live again. He probably asked, "What is the advantage in suffering death when we are fully obedient to God in the observance of his commandment?" From the perplexity of the question an answer came. Those who suffered martyrdom would be raised to a life of happiness on earth ruled by the "saints of the Most High." On the other hand, the apostate Jews and the Syrians who killed them would be raised to endure punishment. Daniel makes no provision for those who live mediocre lives. Resurrection is confined to the extremely good and the extremely bad.

When the doctrine of resurrection emerged in Judaism, the apocalyptists were the originators, developers, and propagators of it. Speculations on the kind of body raised (whether physical or spiritual), divisions of the temporary abode in Sheol, and the final abode of the righteous and wicked occupied the interest of the apocalyptists from the Maccabean period to the second century A.D. The resurrection from the dead became a central tenet of the Pharisees, but their counterpart, the Sadducees, refused to accept the teaching and leaned more toward the skepticism displayed in Ecclesiastes.

Shortly after the teaching of the resurrection from the dead surfaced, questions were introduced concerning the plight of the righteous and the wicked while they were in Sheol. The picture of the situation of the departed is clearly described in 1 Enoch 22:9-13. The author presents us with three compartments in the realm of the dead. One place is reserved for the righteous in which there is a "bright spring of water." Another is the section where the sinners are confined. These sinners are those who have not received punishment for their sins in this life. They will suffer torment while in Sheol. When they are raised from the dead, their pain, suffering, and punishment will continue forever. The third classification by Enoch includes those who are unrighteous but have received punishment for their sins in this life. They will not be raised, but annihilation is their lot. Jesus' parable of the rich man and Lazarus (Luke 16:19-26) gives a picture of the two divisions in Sheol. Lazarus is found in the section reserved for the righteous, while the rich man is in torment in the place reserved for the wicked.

Coupled with the teaching of Sheol, the temporary abode for all who die, is the teaching of Gehenna. The origin of the name and also the idea comes from Ge Hinnom (the valley of Hinnom), a valley to the west of Jerusalem. The Jews used the valley for a garbage dump. The rubbish was always on fire. It was a place where "the worm dies not and the fire is not quenched." The phrase "to be cast into Gehenna" probably meant nothing more in the beginning than something to be discarded as useless. But Gehenna was combined with the Persian notions of a refining fire at the Last Day when Ahura Mazda would purify the people and remove all dross. While the apocalyptists rejected the Persian idea of purification, they used the fire symbol as a form of punishment.

Another feature of apocalyptic teaching is historical dualism. Before the Exile, the Jews believed that God was responsible for everything that happened, whether good or evil. They did not think in terms of second causes. Only when they accepted a dualistic theory did they understand that the world was in the clutches of Satan and the demonic. No doubt this brought great relief to their minds. No longer did they hold to the view that all oppression came from a vengeful God. The temporary rule of evil under Satan and demonic powers brought the vast amount of suffering and misfortune to God's people, but in the end evil could not stand against God's power.

In postexilic Judaism there are three references to the figure Satan. He does not appear in any other portions of the Old Testament. (1) In the book of Job, Satan is presented as one of the sons of God. The name means "adversary." He is a supernatural being who is part of God's heavenly court. His function is that of a prosecuting attorney who tests people to discover if they are as good as they seem to be. If they are not good, Satan can accuse them before God. (2) In Zechariah 3:1-9, Satan appears as a prosecutor, accusing Joshua of not being fit for the high-priesthood. Joshua is exonerated by an angel of God, and Satan is proved to be a false accuser. (3) A later development of the idea of Satan is in 1 Chronicles 21:1. The Chronicler rewrites the story of David taking the census of Israel recorded in 2 Samuel 24:1. In the Samuel story, God entices David to take the census, and then punishes David and the people for the act. The Chronicler attributes the enticement to Satan. Here Satan seems to be an enemy of God, whereas in the other references he is only an enemy of people.

It is still a moot question whether or not the Jews borrowed the idea of Satan from Zoroastrianism while they were under Persian rule. In Persian religion Ahura Mazda, the god of light, and Angra Mainyu, the god of darkness, were in perpetual conflict with each other. Ultimately, Ahura Mazda overcame his bitter enemy Angra Mainyu. If it is not so evident that the Old Testament writers, mentioned above, adopted this concept from the Iranians, it is quite obvious the apocalyptists did. In their writings he is given other names. He is Beliar, Mastema, and Azazel. By whatever name he is called, he is the embodiment of all that is in opposition to God and to human beings.

In contrast to the Old Testament, in which there is not a single demon, the New Testament contains a multitude of demons and demon-possessed people. How do we account for the demons? When did they become realities with whom humanity must contend? We find our answers in apocalyptic literature.

A myth, based upon Genesis 6:1-4, was used by 1 Enoch and Jubilees to explain the origin of demons. The angels in heaven looked down and saw that the daughters of men were fair and beautiful. Consequently, they came down to earth, urged on by lust, and had sexual intercourse with them. The author of 1 Enoch said there were two hundred of them, led by Semyaza (6:1ff.). From this unnatural intercourse a race of giants came into existence. The giants were destroyed by the flood, but their spirits became the demons. Most of the evil spirits were bound by the angels of God, but those who escaped led people astray and caused them to commit all sorts of sins. Ultimately, the demons and Satan (in Jubilees Mastema) will be doomed at the final judgment, but in the meantime they are permitted to carry on their evil activities against humanity.

Another teaching that entered Judaism by way of the apocalyptists during this period was the active role of angels in the affairs of humanity. The Hebrews knew about angels long before the Exile, but it was not until they returned from the Babylonian captivity that angels became realities significantly influential in their daily religious life. The conception of divine transcendence and God's aloofness from the world and human life, noticeable in the Persian period, developed into a problem for the Jews of the Hellenistic age. They were forced to make use of angels to bridge the gap between them and God. It is also possible that out of their reverence for God they thought it might be a discredit to the majesty of God to attribute to God a concern for the petty affairs of people. Therefore, the divine will with respect to such things was performed through the intermediary action of angels.

Angels, who in pre-exilic days were nothing more than manifestations of God's majesty, now became the channels by which God communicated to God's people. The new emphasis on angelic activity in the religion of Israel must have come through Persian influence. The angels ministered to people in various ways. They were guardians of individuals and the nation (Michael was the prince of Israel), intercessors in behalf of humanity before God, communicators of God's message to individuals, and essential participants in the great eschatological drama. From apocalyptic literature we learn that archangels such as Uriel, Raphael, Michael, Gabriel, Remiel, Raguel, and Saraquel functioned with specific assignments. In addition to the archangels, there were thousands upon thousands of subordinate angels who were in the court of heaven to carry out the divine will. There were also the fallen angels who had rebelled against God's authority. These were to suffer punishment on the day of judgment.

In the Old Testament no angel is named except in the book of Daniel where we discover Gabriel and Michael. In this age the unnamed angels assumed distinct personalities. While only seven are clearly identified by name such as the archangels, the multitude of angels were well-defined persons. In the New Testament we find only two of the archangels mentioned: Gabriel and Michael. In Luke's Gospel, Gabriel appears before Zechariah to announce the birth of

John the Baptist (1:19) and before Mary to declare the birth of Jesus (1:26). Jude alludes to the Assumption of Moses in which is related the contention between the archangel Michael and the devil over the body of Moses (v. 9). Michael appears before us again in the book of Revelation expelling Satan from heaven (12:7f).

In the apocalyptic writings frequent use is made of the notion of Paradise. Paradise is a word of Persian origin that means a garden or orchard. In the Septuagint, the Greek translation of the Old Testament, the Hebrew word *gan* (garden) is translated *paradeisos*. The same word is used to translate the garden of Eden in Genesis 2:8, but nowhere in the Old Testament does the word occur in connection with the future abode of the righteous. Paradise is found three times in the New Testament. In Luke's account of the crucifixion, Jesus says to the repentant thief on the cross, "Today you will be with me in Paradise" (23:43). In 2 Corinthians 12:4, the apostle Paul, in defense of his authority, resorts to visions. He said that fourteen years ago he had a vision and was caught up into the third heaven, which was paradise. The third reference is in Revelation 2:7 where the promise is given to the faithful in Ephesus that they would have the privilege of eating of the tree of life "that is in the paradise of God."

It is undeniable, then, that a development of the concept of paradise took place in the apocalyptic period, and this developed form had a considerable influence on New Testament writers. Paradise (the garden of Eden) articulates a correspondence between the beginning time and the end time. Just as Adam and Eve lived in the garden of Eden in God's first creation, in like manner at the end time the righteous will again enjoy a life of primeval happiness and peace in God's new creation. Thus, the end time will be as the beginning. We may say it is from Eden to Eden.

At times paradise, which is to appear at the end of the age takes on an earthly nature.[1] At other times it assumes a heavenly nature and is specified as the abode of the righteous.[2] Quite frequently, the heavenly paradise joins in the character of both the transcendental and the earthly. In 1 Enoch, paradise is situated in the third heaven and has the semblance of the garden of Eden (42:3).

Closely akin to the concept of the return of paradise at the end of the age is that of the heavenly Jerusalem. Both were prepared beforehand by God at the beginning of creation (Apocalypse of Baruch 4:2-6). In this chapter of Baruch we notice that glimpses of the heavenly Jerusalem were given to Abraham and Moses. In the Testaments of the Twelve Patriarchs, a document of the second century B.C., the righteous will rest in Eden and rejoice in the new Jerusalem after the destruction of Beliar (Dan 5:12). Apparently, the combination of the new Jerusalem and Eden suggests Jerusalem will be on earth, because verse 13 states that Jerusalem will no longer endure desolation nor captivity "for the Lord will be in the midst of it." In the apocalyptic works of the first century A.D., the old Jerusalem comes down from God out of heaven and is a counterpart of the earthly Jerusalem.[3]

The new Jerusalem as a counterpart of the earthly Jerusalem crops up in the New Testament. In his allegory of Sarah and Hagar in Galatians 4:22-26, the apostle Paul said that Hagar corresponds to the present Jerusalem, but the new Jerusalem is Sarah. Most assuredly the Apostle was acquainted with the apocalyptic teaching concerning the Jerusalem counterpart in heaven. The author of the Epistle to the Hebrews also knew of this belief for he said, "But you have come to Mount Zion and to the city of the living God, the heavenly Jerusalem, and to innumerable angels in festal gathering" (12:22). The more advanced apocalyptic message comes to us in the book of Revelation where the new Jerusalem comes down from God out of heaven (21:2) and is conflated with the return to the garden of Eden (22:1-6). The combining of these two notions is just as confusing and incoherent in this book as it was in the Jewish apocalyptic documents.

Heretofore, we have considered teachings that were introduced to Judaism in this era, but now we turn to a doctrine that was already established. This is the doctrine of the Messiah. With the disruption of the united kingdom of Israel under Rehoboam, it appeared that the works of David and Solomon were in vain. Nevertheless, from that time on, the prophets from the Northern Kingdom and the Southern Kingdom anticipated a reunification of the monarchy under the rule of a descendant of David. Out of this hope arose a teaching about the Messiah.

Messiah means "anointed." The word had been used in the past history of Israel to indicate the authority and close relation of the prophet, priest, and king to Yahweh. In the latter part of the first century B.C., messiah had become a technical term related to a descendant of David.

In the Hellenistic age some of the Jews centered their hopes in a Davidic messiah, while others were more concerned for a golden age in the future and did not stress the importance of a leader to accomplish this. They longed for a period of independence and power, peace and prosperity, rectitude and piety, and justice and brotherly love among human beings. Many of the apocalyptists who believed that Yahweh would intervene in history and relieve the people of oppression were not interested at all in a messiah. A few of the apocalyptists expected some sort of superhuman figure who would come and bring judgment upon the world along with God as evidenced from the Apocalypse of Ezra, 1 Enoch, and the Apocalypse of Baruch.

Those Jews who anticipated a messiah did not entertain any ideas that the Messiah would suffer. No one but a man of extraordinary military strength could possibly fulfil their hopes and aspirations for national restoration. Furthermore, there is no evidence that they expected anything other than a human being as messiah. It is quite true that there were vague notions of a superhuman figure, as we have already noted, but the normal Jewish hopes were in a man.

The phrase "the kingdom of God," which is very common in the New Testament, is not to be found anywhere in the Old Testament or in apocalyptic writings. Nevertheless, the notion of a kingdom, in which the sovereignty of God is yet to be revealed, is fundamental to the teaching of both classes of literature. When God acts in accordance with the divine predetermined plan and overcomes the forces of evil, God will reign supremely and absolutely. This is the ruling principle of the book of Daniel. Through God's intervention, divine sovereignty will be acknowledged by "all peoples, nations, and languages" (7:14), and all will serve God (7:27). In his night visions,

Daniel saw one like a son of man who came to the Ancient of Days (God), and to this son of man was given everlasting dominion (7:13-14). As man in creation was given sovereignty, so now the man from heaven received the gift of sovereignty over the brutish and malicious powers of the world. Daniel later shows us that the man from heaven represents the saints of the Most High, the ideal Israel whose kingdom is forever and through whom God's rule will be exercised. This is a kingdom on earth in which the surviving members of Israel will share along with the extremely good who are raised from the dead.

While Daniel believed that God's sovereignty would be realized here on earth through Israel, other apocalyptists had different views. Sometimes this event takes place gradually, as in Jubilees. In this book there is no catastrophic intervention of God in history, as in Daniel, and no suggestion of a resurrection. The life span of people will be extended until a thousand years (23:27). Some apocalyptists thought of God's rule as a temporary one on earth. In the Apocalypse of Ezra it lasts for 400 years. Others shared no hope for the full sovereignty of God to be realized on earth either permanently or temporarily. This would come only through the creation of a new heaven and a new earth. Wherever the manifestation of God's awesome power occurred, the writers generally believed that it would be a happening in their own lifetime. Thus, the future was then.

From the time of Daniel onward, the visionaries attempted to reinterpret prophecy and calculate the lengths of different eons in history. They were famous for their periodizing history. The author of the third section of 1 Enoch divided human history into ten weeks. Seven of these weeks had passed. The eighth was to be an era of universal righteousness when the saints would rule the earth. The ninth was to be a period of judgment. In the tenth week the former heaven and earth were to pass away and a new heaven was to appear in which the righteous were to live after they were raised from the dead. Another scheme divided history into seven millennia corresponding to the week of creation.

In addition to the use of numbers to periodize history, the apocalyptists employed them to express other ideas. They believed that numbers had meaning and that meaning could be communicated in terms of numbers. One of the recurring numbers in their allegorical arithmetic is 7, which possibly was drawn from the Babylonian astrology. Note, the number 7 occurs no less than 54 times in the book of Revelation. Other numbers used by the apocalyptists were 3, 3½, 4, 10, 12, 70, 90, 400, 666, and 1000.

The apocalyptic writers have been frequently accused of being pessimists. On the surface we get this impression when we read their books. The pace is set in the second chapter of Daniel where the four empires of the world are depicted by the decreasing preciousness of metals signifying the progressive decline of those powers. The fourth empire representing the Greeks is not only bestial but has the capacity of evil the others did not have. But were the apocalyptists pessimists or realists?

The apocalyptists looked to a world steeped in evil, dominated by tyrannical enemies without and godless leaders within their own ranks, and immersed in unprecedented suffering and pain. They believed that the world was under the domination of evil forces. The sponsor of wickedness could be a human figure such as Antiochus Epiphanes, an evil monster called Satan, the devil, Mastema, Beliar, fallen angels, a superhuman demon, or demon-possessed individuals. They saw the world getting worse and worse, but out of the dark clouds they saw a silver lining. In the fixed plan of God when iniquity and corruption had become so intensified, God would break into history in a cataclysmic manner and destroy the wicked. The visionaries faced the reality of the predominance of evil, but they were optimistic in that God would bring order out of chaos.

Apocalyptic literature is saturated with symbolism. Some of the symbolism is derived from the Old Testament, but much of it is drawn from ancient mythology. The same figures, images, and mental pictures appear in book after book, but, because of the adaptation and readaptation of the old symbols, there is no assurance that they have similar meanings in two successive books. Tiamat and Kingu, the two primeval monsters of chaos in Babylonian mythology, are renamed

Behemoth and Leviathan as they are in the Old Testament. These monsters play a significant role in some of the writings.

The tablets of destiny were also mythological symbols that were borrowed from the Babylonians. The tablets of destiny played a significant role in the Babylonian New Year ritual in the ceremony of deciding the destinies of individuals. In Jubilees and the Testaments of the Twelve Patriarchs the tablets of destiny become the heavenly tablets. In the Jewish apocalyptic writings the idea of destiny is closely akin to the heavenly tablets, but the closest association is in the book of Revelation. There the Lamb is the only one who can take the scroll from God and break its seals (5:6-10). In addition to symbols derived from foreign sources, the writers made great use of animal figures of all sorts to symbolize people and nations. We encounter bears, lions, eagles, leopards, bulls, wolves, dogs, hyenas, foxes, falcons, vultures, ravens, rams, sheep, serpents, and swine.

From Daniel to the seer on Patmos, all of the visionary authors looked forward to a great time of judgment at the end of history. At times judgment is the day that precedes the inauguration of the glorious age, and at other times it begins at the close of this period and initiates the age to come. Sometimes the judgment is made against the Gentiles, and they are destroyed. At other times the apostate Jews and the Gentiles are judged and punished. Sometimes the judgment is restricted to nations, and at other times the judgment falls on demons, Satan, and the fallen angels. At times the judgment has the catastrophic element, and at other times it has the forensic element. In whatever manner it is viewed the final judgment is the concluding act of God in which God's eternal purpose is at last made plain.

Apocalyptic writings contained and emphasized the teachings we have examined thus far. The thought expressed by the authors of these works formed a definite element in Judaism, yet is not clear how widespread the influence was. Some of the religious ideas were accepted by the Pharisees and found their way into rabbinical literature. Another sect in Judaism, the Zealots, doubtless discovered in this genre of literature the religious fanaticism necessary to fan the smoldering coals of nationalism into flames of insurrection. In a sense what they did was contrary to the teachings of these writings that contemplated a divine intervention to deliver the nation. Perhaps they remembered that Daniel had said Judas Maccabeas was a "little help," and they wanted to give God a hand.

It does not seem likely that the Sadducees were at all inclined to embrace the ideas of the apocalyptists. They were opposed to the teachings of angels and demons, and they rejected the notion of the resurrection of the dead. The Essenes, an ascetic group in Judaism who inhabited the desert on the western side of the Dead Sea, went all out for apocalypticism. We have already referred to the work of Josephus, the Jewish historian of the first century A.D., in which he listed some of the teachings of the sect. Furthermore, the abundance of apocalyptic materials discovered in and around the community of Qumran indicates that the sect was fascinated by the writings.

The authors of this fanciful and weird literature were not ignorant and unlearned men. They possessed a depth of knowledge of the Pentateuch and the prophets. Their acquaintance with the alien mythologies is undeniable, yet they used these materials to express their deep faith in their own religion. Their descriptive powers are beyond measure no matter how fantastic, freakish, and irrational they seem. While the Apocalypse of Ezra says that these books were delivered to the wise, they most assuredly had a profound influence on the am ha aretz (the people of the land). There is no doubt about the popularity of these writings among the Jewish people, just as the same popularity manifests itself among many Christians today.

How did rabbinical Judaism respond to this sort of literature? The thought of these literary works reflects ideas of religious circles that were outside the recognized rabbinical schools. This mode of reasoning was in conflict with the scholastic orthodoxy of the Pharisees. The Pharisees were more interested in stressing the demands of God as were the prophets. They built a hedge around the Torah (Law) and fixed a sharp line of demarcation between Israel and the outside world. We have no evidence to support the claim that the rabbis banned these literary works. Perhaps they just ignored them. We must admit, however, that some of the teachings of the apocalyptists profoundly influenced orthodox Judaism, such as the resurrection from the dead, which became an integral part of Judaism.

Jehuda ha-Nasi, the compiler of the oral tradition of the rabbis in the latter part of the second century A.D., was very much opposed to apocalyptic literature, yet he incorporated in his text what might be called a "little apocalypse."[4] Apparently, a chief reason for the rabbis' reaction to the visionaries was their prediction of the end of the age. Rabbi Jonathan ben Eleazer, a Palestine teacher of the third century A.D., is quoted in the Babylonian Talmud as saying, "May they perish who calculate ends; for they said, as soon as the end is reached, and He (Messiah) has not come, he will not come any more."[5]

All elements of the end of days were shattered through a series of events in Jewish history. In A.D. 6, the insurrection of Judas the Galilean was squelched, the revolution of A.D. 66–70 terminated with the destruction of Jerusalem and the temple, and Bar Kokba—hailed as Messiah by the great rabbi Akiba—was killed along with his army in the war against the emperor Hadrian from A.D. 132–135. Consequently, the Jews settled down and concentrated on the study of the Torah. The teachings of the Apocalypse of Ezra, written shortly after the destruction of Jerusalem in A.D. 70 and the repetition of the same ideas in the Apocalypse of Baruch produced soon thereafter, could not survive the disillusionment in the fall of Jerusalem and the defeat of Bar Kokba.

Along with the reaction of rabbis to apocalyptic writings, we observe that some began to object to theosophic teachings (an attempt to have mystical contact with God). A rabbi of the third century A.D. wanted to discard the book of Ezekiel because the earlier chapters of Ezekiel might lead to theosophical speculations. At one time the first chapters of Genesis and Ezekiel were restricted to readers until they reached the age of thirty. During the Middle Ages, theosophical speculations and apocalyptic thought were revived by cabbalistic Judaism. The source for their mystical reveries was the Zohar composed by Moses de Leon. The Zohar was a running commentary on the Pentateuch.

Some of the apocalyptic teachings found their way into Jewish liturgical texts. In them are seen the heavenly bliss of the righteous, the resurrection from the dead, the heavenly banquet, the coming of judgment, the fires of Gehenna, the coming of the new Jerusalem, the birth pangs of the messianic age, and wonders and signs of the last days. Some of the features of these teachings were retained in Jewish literature such as the Midrash, Mishnah, the Talmuds, and the musaf services of Rosh Hashanah and Yom Kippur.

We will now move from our study of this genre of literature that arose in Judaism in the second century B.C. and consider the effect it had in the shaping of Christian thought. While the Gospels were not written before most of the epistles, it seems appropriate to begin with them.

Notes

[1] *The Testaments of the Twelve Patriarchs*, Levi 18:10f.

[2] 2 Enoch 8:1ff; the Apocalypse of Baruch 4:3; 51:11; and the Apocalypse of Ezra 6:26; 7:28, 36ff.; 13:52; 14:9, 49.

[3] The Apocalypse of Baruch 4:3; 32:2-4; the Apocalypse of Ezra 7:26; 8:52f.; 10:44-59; 13:36.

[4] *Mishnah*, Sotah 9:15.

[5] *Sanhedrin* 92b, 97b, 99.

Chapter 4

APOCALYPTIC ELEMENTS
IN THE GOSPELS AND ACTS

The epistles of Paul antedated Mark, our earliest Gospel, by at least twenty years. Therefore, Paul undoubtedly gives us the earliest insights into the life and thought of the primitive Christian community. It is reasonable, however, to assume the Gospels were firmly supported by earlier oral or written sources in Aramaic or Greek, for they were removed in space and time from the environment and generation they set down in writings. In his letters, the apostle Paul was not primarily concerned with the life of the historical Jesus. His chief interest was in an interpretation of the tradition he had received from the Christian community. We begin with the Gospels for the simple reason they present the life, works, and teachings of Jesus.

The Synoptic Gospels

We shall consider the apocalyptic elements in the synoptic Gospels first, because the Fourth Gospel since the time of Clement of Alexandria has been set apart in a class by itself. Clement called it a spiritual Gospel. It was written independently of the sources used by the writers of the other Gospels. In the Fourth Gospel we find devotional paraphrases and expansions of Jesus' words and deeds that indicate theological interpretations.

In dealing with apocalyptic thought in the synoptic Gospels, we shall accept the conclusions of modern scholarship relative to source criticism. Mark is the earliest Gospel, written shortly after the destruction of Jerusalem in A.D. 70. Matthew and Luke followed the outline of Mark and inserted material drawn from another source called Q. The Q source is not extant. It is only arrived at by comparing the citations of Matthew and Luke. At times Matthew omits material recorded by Luke and vice versa. In addition to the use of Matthew and Luke or Mark and the Q source, both Matthew and Luke employ elements peculiar to each.

We are also cognizant of the possibility that the early Christian community shaped the tradition to conform to its interests, thoughts, and needs. The theological stance of the author must be taken into consideration as well. Did he make interpretations of his own?

However, this procedure of starting with the community interpretations, moving on to the sources, and finally examining the author's perspective does not open the door to utter subjectivity. The competency of this approach is acceptable only if substantiated by definite reasons.

Since we have several versions of the sayings of Jesus, it is very easy to see that an apocalyptic element has been included in some of them. This is especially true of Matthew. Most scholars believe that Matthew introduced apocalyptic ideas in his interpretation of two of the parables in chapter 13 of his Gospel. His interest in the parable of the weeds and the parable of the drag net is noteworthy. It is not likely that Jesus explained the two parables in apocalyptic terms. Interestingly, Matthew did not add an interpretation to the parables of the leaven, mustard seed, the hidden treasure, the priceless pearl, or the householder. Perhaps he did not because they could not be subjected to apocalyptic treatment.

Of the eight phrases relating to future punishment and the teachings of last things contained in the synoptic Gospels, forty-four of these appear in Matthew, five in Luke, and five in Mark. The preponderance of the use of these phrases by Matthew makes us believe that he was inclined to supply apocalyptic notions that were not in the teachings of Jesus. Of particular interest is the manner in which Matthew uses "the little apocalypse" in Mark 13.

The setting for the "little apocalypse" in Mark 13 follows Jesus' denunciation of the Pharisees and his observation of the poor widow who put two *lepta* in the temple treasury. In Luke the teaching is placed in the same context as Mark, but Matthew inserts the "little apocalypse" after Jesus had given his lament over Jerusalem (23:37-38). Luke records the lament much earlier in Jesus' departure from Galilee to Jerusalem (13:34-35). In all three accounts Jesus and his disciples left the temple and made their way toward the Mount of Olives. As they passed through the gates of the city and entered the valley of Kidron, all eyes were focused on the colossal irregularly spaced stones in the temple that must have given an impression of almost impregnable strength. We can hear his disciples (Mark says disciple) exclaiming, "What an imposing pile of stone. How magnificent are those buildings!" If the disciples anticipated a response in kind or an expression exceeding their own description, they did not get it. Jesus quickly replied with a prediction of the destruction of the temple. His answer was direct and ominous, "Not one stone will be left here upon another; all will be thrown down" (v. 2).

At first no one made any comment about Jesus' startling announcement. Later while they were all situated on the Mount of Olives where they could see the temple in full view, the disciples pursued the matter. In Mark, the source for the "little apocalypse," the disciples are identified as Peter, James, John, and Andrew. Mark also says that these four disciples asked him a question privately. The question contained two parts, but both parts were related to the subject under discussion—the destruction of the temple (13:4). They wanted to know when the terrible calamity would occur and what the attendant sign might indicate about the imminence of the catastrophe. Matthew, in reviewing Mark 13:5-31, observes that Jesus answered three questions: When will the destruction of the temple happen? What is the sign of Christ's *Parousia* (coming or presence)? What will be the sign of the end of the age? (v. 3)

One of the problems posed by Matthew relative to the disciples' question and Jesus' reply to their inquiry is the author's insertion of the word *Parousia* no less than four times in chapter 24. Etymologically, the word means "being alongside" or "present," but in regular usage it means "presence." As a technical term it could designate the manifestation of a divine person (theophany) or the visit of a royal person. *Parousia* does not appear in any of the other Gospels, though it is found quite frequently in Paul's epistles (1 Cor 15:23; 1 Thess 2:19; 3:13; 4:15; 5:23; 2 Thess 2:1, 8) and in some other epistles (Jas 5:7; 2 Pet 1:16; 3:4, 12; 1 John 2:23). Its prevailing use in the early church was to designate the coming of the risen Christ to his believers after an interval of undetermined length. Matthew followed the expectation of the early church concerning the imminent return of Christ (24:3, 27, 37, 39). He evidently understood that some of the discourse in Mark 13 did not apply to the destruction of the temple but referred to Christ's coming again and the termination of the age.

Before we consider the teaching of Mark 13 and the use that is made of this chapter by Matthew and Luke, it is important for us to determine if the contents represent the teaching of Jesus or if it is a document that was composed to warn the Jewish Christians to escape from Jerusalem before its destruction. Since the time of Colani in 1864, who suggested that Mark 13 contained more than the genuine sayings of Jesus, scholars have been suspicious of this chapter.

The suspicions of scholars are aroused for several reasons. (1) Much of the material is foreign to the message of Jesus. Such phrases as "the desolating sacrilege," "but for the sake of the elect," "the sun will be darkened," and "stars will be falling from heaven" seem to be unlike his customary language. (2) This is the only lengthy discourse of Jesus in the Gospel of Mark. It is even longer than the collection of parables in chapter 4. (3) The words, "Let the reader understand" (v. 14), seem to be very unusual in light of the fact that the words were spoken by Jesus and not written. It is impossible to say that the reference is to Daniel because Mark does not mention this book. It is Matthew who adds Daniel in his account.

From Eusebius,[1] the father of church history who lived in Caesarea in the fourth century, we learn that an oracle circulated among the Jewish Christians just before the siege of Jerusalem. The nature of the oracle was a warning for the Jewish Christians to leave the city of Jerusalem and flee to Pella, one of the cities of the Decapolis on the east side of the river Jordan.

As we have noted before, in this discourse, Jesus was supposed to answer a question from his disciples that had to do with the destruction of the temple, yet this is only one of the topics touched on by him. Our problem in interpreting this chapter in Mark and the use of it by Matthew and Luke is the identification of the part of the answer relating to the destruction of the temple and those portions that point toward a future coming of Christ. If this is an oracle similar to the one to which Eusebius alluded, someone has taken out of context some of the sayings Jesus spoke on other occasions in order to give an entirely different impression. Scholars are of the opinion that Mark 13:9-13 are genuine sayings of Jesus. There is general agreement that Mark 13:24-27 and parallels in Matthew and Luke are apocalyptic insertions.

The document injected into Mark's Gospel, which proposes to be an answer from Jesus concerning the destruction of the temple, begins with 13:5 and continues through 13:31. It opens with a warning to the disciples about being led astray by the inevitable appearance of false messiahs, pretenders who would make claims of being deliverers of Israel. The warning was not so much against the deceptive methods of these leaders but against their success in deceiving the people.

When Jesus was but a boy, Judas the Galilean, in A.D. 6, boasted of his greatness as a leader of the Jews in his fight against the Romans. During the reign of Claudius as emperor of Rome, Theudas amassed a large number of followers. To prove that he was the anointed of God as leader of the Jews, he claimed that he could make the waters of the river Jordan part as Joshua did in years gone by (Acts 5:36). Later an Egyptian gathered a company of men around himself and boasted that he could make the walls of Jerusalem fall just as the walls of Jericho tumbled before Joshua and the Israelites. During the Jewish revolt against Rome in A.D. 66-70, John of Gischala, the insurrectionist from Galilee, deceived the Jews into believing he could lead them to victory against the Romans.

Even a cursory reading of Mark 13 will reveal a repetition of verses 5 and 6 in verses 21-23. The latter verses make it more clear that false messiahs will arise.

The document continues with Jesus admonishing his disciples about connecting his return with economic, political, domestic, and forces of nature they might encounter. They will hear reports of wars among nations, earthquakes, famines, and many other disasters, but these sufferings do not indicate in any way the return of Christ. The disciples must not allow their eager desire for the termination of the age to betray them into a premature belief that the end is near. These troubles portend only the beginning of sufferings. They are what normally happen in world history.

In Mark 13:8, "the beginning of the birth pangs" was a well-known Jewish apocalyptic and rabbinical phrase for the pains, ills, and troubles that must precede the age to come. The teachings probably grew out of a belief that people who were in pain and suffering might express a greater faith in God. In the book of Jubilees 23:18-19 and the Apocalypse of Baruch 27–29, the birth pangs of the age to come are described in details resembling what we find in the synoptic Gospels. Both of these are Jewish apocalyptic works; the former was written in the second century B.C., and the latter in the first century A.D.

The additional kinds of suffering were related to the Christian community (13:9-13). There seems to be no doubt as to the genuineness of these verses coming from Jesus, but they could have been given on a previous occasion. This seems evident from Matthew's inclusion of some of them in his Gospel where there is another setting (10:17-21). The crises Jesus' followers would face included persecution, floggings in synagogues, appearances before rulers to defend themselves for their witnessing, and betrayals in family relationships that could bring death.

Matthew adds to the account of Mark other elements of danger within the Christian community (24:10-14). There would be apostasy—many who believed in Christ would fall away. Christians would betray Christians. False prophets would arise within the community. Love for Christ and presumably love for a fellow Christian were doomed to wane. Despite the persecution from without and unfaithfulness within, nothing could stop the spreading of the good news until the whole inhabited world was reached. According to Matthew's Gospel, the termination of the age will be after the good news has been proclaimed throughout the whole world. Perhaps Mark 13:10, "And the good news must first be proclaimed to all nations," was understood by Matthew to be an extension of time before the end of the age. It is very noticeable, though, that Mark does not say the end of the age will come as soon as the gospel has been proclaimed to all nations. This is another example of Matthew's interest in apocalyptic.

Jesus' forecast of the destruction of the temple disturbed the disciples, and they were anxious to know when the event would occur. Jesus' discourse up to this point contained nothing related to the temple. Only when we read Mark 13:14 do we get a hint about the destruction of the temple. Without Luke's interpretation of "the desolating sacrilege," we would never understand this section in Mark or the equivalent in Matthew as a reference to the destruction of Jerusalem. Luke, who wrote after the fall of Jerusalem, interpreted "the desolating sacrilege" as the siege of the Holy City by the Romans in A.D. 70. "When you see Jerusalem surrounded by armies, then know that its desolation has come near" (Luke 21:20). Previously, Luke had recorded Jesus' prediction of the destruction of Jerusalem just after his entry into Jerusalem in chapter 19. Some of the Pharisees asked Jesus to rebuke his disciples who were shouting, "Blessed is the king who comes in the name of the Lord." Jesus refused to do it, and as he came near the city of Jerusalem, he wept over it and said, "Indeed, the days will come upon you, when your enemies will set up ramparts around you and surround you, and hem you in on every side" (19:43).

Matthew considers the special sign for the disciples to flee from Jerusalem to be found in "the desolating sacrilege" that will stand in the holy place (the temple). He clarifies the meaning of the phrase by reference to its source in the book of Daniel. In Daniel, the appalling horror (9:27; 12:11) was the desecration of the temple by Antiochus Epiphanes in 168 B.C. The Syrian king ordered the statue of Zeus to be erected in the temple area and constructed an altar for Zeus upon which swine were sacrificed. Many of the Jews were on the verge of revolting against Rome when Gaius Caligula, in A.D. 40, ordered his statue to be placed in the temple. Christians may have seen in this act of Caligula a repetition of the blasphemy of Antiochus Epiphanes. To be sure, the curious phrase can stand for any evil person who would force a horrible conflict between good and evil, but it seems evident that Matthew has in mind the desecration of the temple by the Romans in A.D. 70.

All three of the synoptic Gospels relate what the disciples are to do when the impending crisis comes. They must get out of the city of

Jerusalem and the province of Judea without delay. If a person is on the housetop repairing the roof or taking a nap, he or she should not take time to gather up household possessions before running. If a man is plowing in the field or sowing his crop, he must leave his cloak behind and not delay his flight by searching for it. On that day it will be extremely difficult for the pregnant women and those with small children to escape because they will be handicapped in their exodus. If the flight is during the winter, they might face the threat of flooded wadis and rivers. Matthew betrays his Jewishness by adding that the escapees should pray that the day of the flight might fall on a day other than the Sabbath. There will be no time for pious observance of Sabbath regulations for limited distance of travel on that day.

Matthew, Mark, and Luke describe this event as a time of distress, misery, and anguish. Mark, followed by Matthew, says, "For in those days there will be such suffering, such as has not been from the beginning of the creation that God created until now, and never will be" (13:19). Luke adds, "They will fall by the edge of the sword and be taken away as captives among all nations" (21:24). Indeed the sufferings of the Jews, in A.D. 70, were horrible beyond belief. To get the details of this holocaust, one only has to read Josephus *Wars of the Jews*, Books VI and VII. From outside the city, Titus and the Romans bombarded Jerusalem with tremendous stones while laying siege to the city, and within Jerusalem, the Jews were fighting among themselves.

Mark and Matthew, writing after the destruction of Jerusalem, insert a note stating that unless the days of this conflict had been shortened, no human being would have been spared. But the bloody conflict came to an end after a short period of time "for the sake of the elect." Matthew still views this as a future event, even though he knew that it had happened when he wrote. He says, "Those days will be cut short" (24:22). Luke on the other hand says, "Jerusalem will be trampled on by the Gentiles, until the times of the Gentiles are fulfilled" (21:24). What did he mean by this? Perhaps the statement is similar to the shortening of the days, and he meant until the time the Romans had completed their destruction of Jerusalem.

Jesus was not the first one to forecast an awful fate for the temple. Micah had envisaged the destruction of the first temple because Israel had refused to repent (3:12). Many years later Jeremiah echoed the same prediction (26:6). For Jeremiah, it was a more imminent threat due to the rising power of the Babylonian empire. In 586 B.C., he saw his predictions come true when Jerusalem and the temple fell.

There seems to be no doubt that Jesus declared a coming catastrophe for the temple. If he had not done so, we would not have the garbled testimony put forth by the two witnesses at his trial before Caiaphas, the high priest (Mark 14:57-58 and Matthew's parallel). At the crucifixion the crowd shouted, "Aha! You who would destroy the temple and build it in three days, save yourself" (Mark 15:29). Jesus' forecast was in part based upon the observation of historic forces he could see at work. He blamed the leaders who could predict the weather but could not interpret the present time (Luke 12:56). He believed that if the Jews persisted in their reactionary attitude toward Rome, they would perish just as the Galilean whose blood Pilate mingled with their sacrifices or the eighteen people upon whom the tower of Siloam fell (Luke 13:1-4). Israel's fanaticism was on a collision course with Rome. By giving diligence to a change in attitude, the nation could avert a foreseen disaster.

Embedded in the "little apocalypse" of Mark 13 is a full apocalyptic section that is considered alien to the teachings of Jesus (24–27). It contains material suggested by Isaiah 13:10, Daniel 7:13-14, Zechariah 6:6; 12:12, and Isaiah 27:12-13. In the Mark passage we notice that the powers of heaven will be shaken, the Son of man coming on the clouds of heaven and sending out his angels to gather the elect from the ends of earth to the ends of heaven. Matthew adds the trumpet call of the angels (24:31) and makes it more of a time that ends all time. Mark 13:30, which is still part of the discourse, has Jesus saying, "Truly, I tell you, this generation will not pass away until all these things have taken place." It seems that the future was then.

The utterance in Mark 13:32 is a reply to a question, but we do not know what the question is in the immediate context. The verse says, "But about that day or hour no one knows, neither the angels in heaven, nor the Son, but only the Father." How shall we interpret "that day"? To what does it refer? In Luke's Gospel "that day" is an allusion to the destruction of Jerusalem (17:21). Presumably Matthew understood "that day" to mean the end of the age.

Remember, many scholars believe that Mark 13:5-31 is a written document inserted into the Gospel. Based on this assumption, Mark 13:32 is the answer to the question of the disciples concerning the destruction of the temple. Jesus simply said that he did not know the time.

Matthew is not content with just the apocalyptic elements in the "little apocalypse" on Mark. He departs from Mark and follows the Q source, joining it with the "little apocalypse." The Q source material in Luke comes in chapters 17 and 21. In Luke the passages have no connection with the termination of the age or the *parousia* (the early church's teaching concerning the return of Christ). In light of the promise of Christ's return, Matthew stresses the urgency of watchfulness (24:27-51). He further emphasizes the pressing importance of the spirit of alertness in Chapter 25. Since Jerusalem had fallen before Matthew wrote, and Christ had not yet returned, to what duties should Christians apply themselves while they waited for his coming? Matthew adds three parables that are not found in the other Gospels. They seem to be an answer to the above question. The three parables are the ten maidens, the talents, and the last judgment.

The age of Jesus was submerged in apocalyptic speculations, but Jesus introduced a bare minimum of apocalyptic imagery. Even that bare minimum might be reduced more so when we discount those ingredients that may have been added by the authors of the synoptic Gospels. His mission was to invoke an ultimate endorsement of his own word and works. The core of Jesus' teaching centered around what God was actually doing in and through him. It was faith in the risen Lord that opened up the way for apocalyptic elaboration in the early Christian community. The New Testament epistles reveal how far apocalyptic eschatology had permeated the Christian fellowship. Even in the epistles it is not apocalyptic fantasy that is unrestrained.

Assuredly, God did break into the world in Jesus Christ who was God incarnate. Yet God's breaking into the world was unlike the apocalyptists who visualized it as an act of destruction. It is an unmistakable fact of history that when Jesus entered the process of human life, a spiritual power, unparalleled in scope, was released. Into a world saturated with evil there came silently a new regenerating force greater than the apocalyptist could ever imagine.

The Fourth Gospel

The author of the Fourth Gospel gives no indication anywhere in his writing that he was influenced by apocalyptic eschatology. He perceives that through the incarnation of God in Jesus a New Age had dawned in human history. The coming of the Son of Man on the clouds of glory so explicitly promised in the "little apocalypse" of the synoptic Gospels as an external event is transmuted to a spiritual communion by John. By the time John's Gospel was written at the close of the first century A.D. the return of Christ, the resurrection, and the final judgment were firmly fixed in the tradition of the Christian community. It appears, however, that John detached the essential truth of Christianity from the apocalyptic eschatological hope of the primitive church. In John we discover that Jesus returned to his followers in the mission of the *Paraclete* (the comforter, counselor, or advocate). Paul before the Areopagus in Athens said, "He [God] has fixed a day on which he will have the world judged in righteousness by a man whom he has appointed, and of this he has given assurance to all by raising him from the dead" (Acts 17:31). For John, however, the final judgment is taking place continuously in the here and now. He did not rule out a consummation of history because he wrote about "the last day" (12:48) and a resurrection for judgment for those who have been evil (5:29).

As to the resurrection, in chapter 5, John records these words of Jesus: "Truly, I tell you, anyone who hears my word and believes him who sent me has eternal life, and does not come into judgment, but has passed from death to life" (5:24). This saying is followed by "The hour is coming, and is now here, when the dead will hear the voice of the Son of God, and those who hear will live" (v. 25). In the first citation God's deliverance is not in the future as something hoped for but offered now in Christ, and those who believe have eternal life as a present possession. In the second citation the present hour is the one in which those who hear and believe have passed from death to life. In addition to the hour that "is now here," the author goes on to record, "For the hour is coming when all who are in their graves will hear his voice and will come out" (vv. 28-29a). Thus John presents a resurrection in two stages: "the now time" and "the time to come." It seems quite clear that the first stage in John is far more important than the second.

Another passage in John where Jesus discusses resurrection from death is found in chapter 11 relative to the death of Lazarus. Jesus was on the other side of the river Jordan when he told his disciples that Lazarus had died. He and his disciples made the journey to Bethany near Jerusalem. When Martha, the sister of Lazarus, heard that Jesus was coming, she went out to meet him. She was confident that her brother would not have died if Jesus had been present. Jesus assured her that her brother would rise again, and she countered with her apocalyptic hopes of a resurrection on the last day. Jesus then said, "I am the resurrection and the life. Those who believe in me, even though they die, will live, and everyone who lives and believes in me will never die" (11:25-26). Jesus raised Lazarus from the tomb to show that he, in this life, had the power over life and death. Thus the apocalyptic hopes of the people can be realized in the here and now. Not only was it a dramatic act to illustrate the truth of the declaration in chapter 5; it was a mighty work to manifest his own death and resurrection, which to John was one of the greatest signs.

One of the reasons why primitive Christianity adopted the teaching that Christ would return was because he suffered humiliation in his crucifixion, and this had to be rectified by a coming with majesty, power, and glory to validate the fact that he was indeed the Messiah. That is why John, contrary to the synoptic Gospels, points to the cross as the ultimate manifestation of God's glory (the revealing of God's character). To be sure, the glory of the cross was climaxed with the resurrection of Jesus. The eruption of the divine order was not connected with a return of Christ but in his incarnation. This is attested to in the prologue of John's Gospel: "And the Word became flesh and lived among us, and we have seen his glory, the glory as of a father's only Son, full of grace and truth" (1:14). The wonder works or miracles (*signs* in John's Gospel to show a spiritual reality behind an act of Jesus that otherwise may be considered a barefaced miracle), the acts and sayings of Jesus at the various Jewish festivals, plus conversations with individuals, all move forward in a dramatic fashion to the final glorification of God in Christ in the crucifixion.

The farewell discourse of Jesus in John's Gospel is of a very different character than that presented to us in the synoptic Gospels (Mark 13 and parallels). True, Jesus spoke of his coming in chapter 14:3, but it is of a different kind. The discourse covers four chapters in the Gospel. Admittedly, some of the material may be interpretations of the author. There are also some repetitions.

Before his departure, Jesus realized that he must comfort his disciples and give them full assurance that even though he was leaving them to go to the Father he would not be absent from them. The contact between heaven and earth that had been effected by Jesus while here on earth would not cease. The communication would be even greater since he would return in the Spirit and guide them. Therefore, Jesus said,

> Do not let your hearts be troubled. Believe in God, believe also in me. In my Father's house there are many dwelling places. If it were not so, would I have told you that I go to prepare a place for you? And if I go and prepare a place for you, I will come again and will take you to myself, so that where I am, there you may be also. (14:1-3)

Were these consoling words related to the immediate present or to a far distant future event? What is the meaning of "abiding place"? What is the meaning of Jesus' coming again?

These words of Jesus could hardly have been helpful to the disciples if some far-off future event was meant. Even for the author these words held no significance, if they could not be applied in the present to demonstrate the superiority of Christianity over Judaism. "My Father's house" was used by Jesus in the second chapter as a reference to the temple. It is quite clear that in 14:2 "my Father's house" does not mean temple. It has to do with God's domain. In the realm of God there are many *monai* (abiding places). The word *mone* is found only two times in the New Testament, and both of these occur in chapter 14 of John's Gospel. The usual translation is "mansion," which is the Latin equivalent of *mone*. Origin, head of the catechetical school in Alexandria, Egypt, in the third century A.D., quoted John 14:2f. and understood *monai* (plural of *mone*) as stations on the way to God.

In addition to "my Father's house" and "abiding places," another word should be considered in the message of Jesus. This is the word *topos*, which means "place." In chapter 11, the chief priests and Pharisees gathered a council together to decide what they should do with Jesus. They feared that if they allowed Jesus to continue unmolested, he would instigate an insurrection, and the Romans would take away their "holy place and nation" (v. 48). Here "place" is a synonym for the temple. It would seem that John is also using the word *topos* (place) as a synonym for the temple.

In rabbinic tradition the glory of God left the temple just before the Romans under Titus entered the city of Jerusalem to carry out its destruction. The author may have been acquainted with such a tradition, and in this portion of the farewell discourses was trying to show to his readers that the Jews, by rejecting Jesus, forfeited their right to be the people of God. The localized presence of God was now with those who believed in Jesus as Messiah, the Son of God. In earlier portions of this Gospel there were intimations that the localized presence of God no longer would be in the temple in Jerusalem or on Mount

Gerizim in Samaria (4:21f.) True worshipers were to worship the Father in spirit and truth (4:23), and the true sanctuary was Jesus himself (2:19f.). The temple in Jerusalem was the Father's house on earth until the unbelief of the Jews made it desolate.

The many chambers of the temple may have suggested the use of *monai* for the "abiding places" that were in the domain of God. These "abiding places" Jesus will prepare for the disciples, and then he will return to them. He will not leave them orphans but will come to them. That the "abiding-places" are not reserved for the future in heaven is made clear later when Jesus said, "If a man love me, he will keep my word; and my father will love him, and we will come and make our *moné* (abiding place) beside him" (v. 23).

It would seem then that the meaning of chapter 14 is related to an immediate present rather than a distant future experience. The new presence of God is not to be discovered in mortar and bricks, but in the individual. Here the presentation of John is similar to that of Paul. "Do you not know that you are God's temple and that God's Spirit dwells in you? . . . For God's temple is holy, and you are that temple" (1 Cor 3:16-17). "Do you not know that your body is a temple (sanctuary) of the Holy Spirit within you, which you have from God?" (1 Cor 6:19). "In him the whole structure is joined together and grows into a holy temple in the Lord; in whom you also are built together spiritually into a dwelling place for God" (Eph 2:21-22).

In chapter 14, John records Jesus' saying three times that he would come to his disciples (vv. 3, 18, 28) and one time that "we will come" (v. 23). Some have interpreted the coming of Jesus as a reference to the resurrection rather than the coming of the Spirit, although there is too close a relation in the discourse between Jesus' coming and the sending of the Paraclete to dissociate the two. In this Gospel the return of Jesus is definitely linked with the sending of the Spirit. The *Paraclete* will be the spiritual presence of Jesus (vv. 15-17); he will continue the work of Jesus; he will bear witness concerning Jesus (15:26-27); he will reprove the world concerning sin, righteousness, and judgment (16:8f); and he will guide the disciples to all truth (16:13).

It appears that John reinterpreted the popular eschatology of the return of Christ by pointing out that the Spirit will abide with the Christians as an assurance of his presence. While John did not rule out a consummation of the age, he did counter the apocalyptic notions, prevalent in his time, of a future coming in a cataclysmic manner.

Acts

If the author of the Gospel and Acts are the same, why is it that a few apocalyptic elements appear in his Gospel, but in Acts we find no definite features of this sort? The tendency of Luke is to omit parables in Q, such as the parables of the weeds and the drag net, that depict this kind of thought. He alone gives the parable of the rich man and Lazarus in which the apocalyptic teaching of division in Sheol is colorfully described. Also at the end of the parable of the unjust judge, he inserts something akin to Revelation 6:9-11. This is secondary to the parable, however. In the "little apocalypse" where he depends on the Marcan source, he revises the material to make it point more toward the destruction of Jerusalem. He did the same for the Q sayings found in his Gospel (17:24-37). Thus, in his Gospel Luke kept the apocalyptic to a bare minimum.

When we examine the book of Acts, it is surprising to discern that there are no apocalyptic traits recorded in the proclamations of the early church. By placing five of the speeches recorded in Acts side by side, we perceive that they follow a certain pattern. The feature we find in all five are: the fulfillment of Old Testament promises, the death of Jesus, the resurrection of Jesus, the offer of forgiveness, and the apostles as witnesses to these things. The five speeches are found in chapters 2, 3, 5, 10, and 13.

The only two references to the return of Christ occur in the early chapters of Acts. One is on the occasion of the ascension. Jesus was lifted up and a cloud intervened removing him from their sight.

While he was going and they were gazing up toward heaven, suddenly two men in white robes stood by them. They said, "Men of Galilee, why do you stand looking up toward heaven? This Jesus, who has been taken up from you into heaven, will come in the same way as you saw him go into heaven." (1:10-11)

The other reference is in the speech of Peter in 3:19-22. Here it seems that the return was contingent on the repentance of the Jews.

No doubt the speeches so delivered were the actual words of each person. If Luke constructed the speeches as historians in his time customarily did, he did so on the basis of what he knew to be primitive preaching. Whether the speeches were recorded as given or whether Luke fashioned them in accord with the proclamation of the early church, the result is the same. The speeches contained no apocalyptic traits. Yet when we read the epistles of Paul and other epistles, the apocalyptic ideas hit us broadside. Was Luke, who made a hero out of Paul in Acts, unacquainted with the epistles of Paul? Perhaps the epistles of Paul had not been collected at the time of his writing of Acts between 80 and 85 A.D. Nevertheless, if Luke was a travel companion of Paul, surely he would know of his teachings about the future. Of course, there are many differences between the Acts account of Paul and the Paul in his epistles. The differences lead us to assume that Luke was not a travel companion of Paul.

Let us now review the epistles of Paul and see if there are apocalyptic traces found in his letters to the various churches he established.

Note

[1] Eusebius, *Eccesiastical History*, III.5.

Chapter 5

APOCALYPTIC ELEMENTS
IN THE EPISTLES

In our examination of Acts we failed to detect any awareness by Luke of apocalyptic ideas in the preaching of the early church, but when we consider the epistles of Paul and the other epistles in the New Testament, there is an abundance of these traits. If Luke records accurately the situation of primitive Christianity, when, how, and for what reasons did the apocalyptic elements become a part of the tradition? Did Luke attempt to idealize the early church and suppress the apocalyptic? Was Paul the originator of the movement to express these notions? If he was responsible, how do we explain the traces of apocalyptic in the other epistles? These are good questions, but the answers to them are beyond our understanding. First, let us inspect the epistles of Paul and then turn to the other epistles.

The Epistles of Paul

The epistles of Paul constitute approximately one-third of the New Testament, and if we add the Pastorals (1 Timothy, 2 Timothy, Titus), there is considerably more. The Pastorals, while they contain fragments of genuine Pauline letters, were written subsequently to the time of Paul under his name. The epistles of Paul about which there is no doubt among scholars are: 1 Thessalonians, 1 and 2 Corinthians, Galatians, Romans, Philippians, and Philemon. Largely because of the apocalyptic teaching in 2 Thessalonians 2:3-12, some deny that 2 Thessalonians is a genuine letter of Paul. Some scholars reject Colossians and Ephesians saying that these come from another hand even though they contain some material consistent with Paul's thinking. We will accept as genuine all of the epistles of Paul with the exception of the Pastorals.

All of the letters of Paul fall within a period of ten or fourteen years (A.D. 50–60), before the fall of Jerusalem. Since his letters are not theological treatises but are more related to pastoral problems in the churches, it is impossible to derive anything such as a constructive theology from them. The only epistle that approaches a system of theology is the one Paul wrote to the Romans. Even here his thoughts center around a right relationship with God by faith in Jesus Christ.

Since the various churches had different problems, Paul is not always consistent in his theological thoughts.

Embedded in Paul's epistles are many traces of apocalyptic ways of expressing matters. Did he get this from the community tradition, or was he influenced by Jewish apocalyptic literature? He could have obtained these ideas from both sources. Before Paul became a Christian, he was a Jew who embraced the teachings of the Pharisee party in Judaism. Some of the teachings of apocalyptists seeped into Pharisaism before the fall of Jerusalem in A.D. 70, but those that did not fit into normative Judaism were ignored. They retained the doctrines of the resurrection from the dead and the two ages (the present age and the age to come), but they allowed angelology and demonology to play a subordinate role in normative Judaism. But since Paul wrote prior to the formation of normative Judaism, it is conceivable that more of the apocalyptic ideas permeated Judaism. If this is true, then Paul received this kind of teaching from his Jewish heritage.

If we had sufficient evidence to classify Paul's epistles in a chronological order, perhaps there would be the possibility of seeing a progression in his manner of thinking. There is a divergence of opinions among scholars relative to the order of the Epistles, however. Even if we could determine the order, this would not preclude the apostle's lapsing into expressions more familiar to him from his Jewish heritage. Without trying to show a development in Paul's reasoning, we will examine the epistles with no particular chronological order in mind.

Paul accepted the doctrine of two ages so frequently set forth in apocalyptic literature. This same teaching was accepted by the rabbis as well. They spoke of this age (*'olam hazzeh*) and the age to come (*'olam habba'*). For Paul, this present age is evil (Gal 1:4) and is under the control of the devil (2 Cor 4:4). If the forces of evil in this age had realized that what they did spelled their doom, they would not have been involved in the crucifixion of Jesus (1 Cor 2:8). In Romans, Paul exhorts the Christians in Rome to be transformed in their minds and not be conformed to the pattern of this age that is dominated by evil (12:2). Again, in 1 Corinthians, Paul says, "For the wisdom of this world is foolishness with God" (3:19). In Ephesians 1:21, the Apostle joins "this age" with the "age to come."

Our struggle in this life, according to Paul, is not so much against people, "but against the rulers, against the authorities, against the cosmic powers of this present darkness, against the spiritual forces of evil in the heavenly places" (Eph 6:12). In Romans 8:38, the angels, powers, and principalities are those evil forces that cannot separate us from the love of God. Rarely does Paul speak of good angels. His reference is to the fallen angels of apocalyptic thought. These powers are spiritual beings, exercising independent rule, and have exceedingly great control over this age. They are to be identified with "the rulers of this age" (1 Cor 2:8). The chief of these spiritual powers hostile to God is Satan (2 Cor 12:7; 1 Cor 5:5).

Paul conceives of the Christian community as a small stronghold in the midst of the hostile forces of evil. In Philippians 3:20, he likens the community to a colony of heaven. We are situated in a foreign land among enemies. To turn a person out of the community is the equivalent of putting that person in the camp of Satan (1 Cor 5:5). To restore such a one means that Satan is deprived of the advantage he has gained (2 Cor 2:11). The dirty works of Satan are to hinder, weaken, and nullify the work of God (1 Thess 2:18; 2 Thess 3:3; Rom 16:20). The god of this world (Satan) blinds the minds of unbelievers to prohibit them from seeing the light of the good news of the glory of Christ (2 Cor 4:4). Satan is a tempter (1 Cor 7:5; 1 Thess 3:5; 2 Cor 11:3). According to 2 Thessalonians 2:8ff., Satan becomes incarnate in a person, but his evil and cunning disguise are thwarted because Jesus slays him with the breath of his mouth.

Whether or not we believe there exists a person named Satan, Beliar, Mastema, the dragon, the serpent, or whatever, we are certainly cognizant of malevolent, sinister, and nefarious energies that block our paths on the way to do the will of God. There is an external power that entices us. In following the apocalyptic teaching of Satan, demons, and fallen angels, Paul lays the blame on these external forces for the ills of the world. Occasionally, he falls back on his rabbinic leanings and ignores the external powers. In Roman 7:13-25, he takes up the teaching of the rabbis concerning the *yetzer ha tov* (the good inclination or impulse) and the *yetzer ha ra'* (the evil inclination or impulse). There is an internal battle being waged in the individual between good and evil. Paul gives thanks to God because the principle of the Spirit of life delivered him from the evil impulse within.

Paul learned of a problem existing in the church he established in Thessalonica. Some of those in the fellowship had quit work because they had understood the Apostle in his teaching, while among them, to indicate that Christ was to return soon. Not only had they ceased working at their jobs, but they were sponging off the others who interpreted Paul's words in a different fashion. In both Thessalonian letters there is a reference to the idlers.

Some scholars, because they see a discrepancy in Paul's reasoning about the *Parousia* (the presence of Christ or manifestation of Christ) in 2 Thessalonians 2:1-12 and 1 Thessalonians 4:13-18, contend that the second letter precedes the first. In the second letter the *Parousia* does not occur until certain signs are observed, while in the first letter the *Parousia* is not related to events that occur before Christ's coming: "For you yourselves know very well that the day of the Lord will come like a thief in the night" (5:2).

Whether or not we accept this order of the two epistles, it is much better to begin with 2 Thessalonians 2:1-12. In this passage Paul employs the prophetic utterances of the Day of Yahweh. Since Christ has been confessed as Lord, he is the same as Yahweh of the Old Testament. Only Yahweh has power over life and death, and since Jesus was raised from the dead, he is *kurios* (Lord), a translation of the Hebrew word for Yahweh by the Greek *kurios*. Thus, Paul can say the *Parousia* of our Lord Jesus Christ and mean by this the coming of Yahweh.

To ward off the false teaching that had come to the church through a forged letter or a word he had spoken to them, Paul warns them that the day of the Lord has not come as some suppose. Then he introduces a Jewish legend of an evil being who would appear in the last days. We can trace it back to Daniel. In Daniel 11:30-37, an evil king will profane the sanctuary, and some of the Jews will be guilty of apostasy. Daniel sees Antiochus Epiphanes as the profaner of the sanctuary who sets himself above every god. Pompey, the Roman general who made the Jews subservient to Rome in 63 B.C., entered the Holy of Holies in the temple of Jerusalem. The Song of Solomon calls him the "insolent one." In A.D. 40, Caligula, the Roman emperor, ordered Petronius, the legate of Syria, to set up his statue in the temple. Caligula wanted to be worshiped as a god. The reaction of the Jews was so intense that he delayed the action. In the meantime, in A.D. 41, Caligula died, so the attempt was aborted. Of course, Paul did not equate Caligula with the "man of lawlessness" because he had been dead for many years.

Paul says that Christ will not return until there is first an apostasy. What does he mean by apostasy? We have noted that Daniel spoke of apostate Jews. To apostatize means to turn away from God. Does apostasy refer to Jews? In the context of both Thessalonian letters we assume that he meant Jews. But who is this man of lawlessness who is about to be unveiled? Paul also calls him the son of perdition. This person "opposes and exalts himself against every so-called god or object of worship, so that he takes his seat in the temple of God, declaring himself to be God" (2 Thess 2:4). Some scholars think the man of lawlessness is a Jew, not a pagan. In this case, it would be the high priest who set himself up as God. To make the high priest the man of lawlessness, however, does not seem likely even if the high priests in the first century A.D. were evil men. Then too, there is no connection of apostasy with the man of lawlessness other than an apostasy will precede the epiphany of the evil one.

Whoever Paul has in mind, he makes it clear that there is a restraining force and a restrainer at the present time to keep the enemy from setting himself up as God. It is possible that the restraining force is the Roman Empire and the restrainer is the Roman emperor Claudius. Perhaps Paul, with the knowledge of what Caligula did, anticipated that a similar action from a future emperor who might arise and would do what Caligula was unable to do.

In this passage we further observe that Paul says there will be a *Parousia* of Christ and a *Parousia* of the lawless one. Satan has energized this man with all power and with false signs and wonders. In fact, he is the incarnation of Satan. Just as the apocalyptists looked to a time when there would be such a concentration of sin and iniquity in the world in one man or in people as a whole, so Paul kept step with them and believed that the end of time was near because the mystery of lawlessness was already at work.

In 2 Thessalonians 1:4-10, Paul breathes out invectives on those who have persecuted and afflicted those of the Christian community in Thessalonica and follows with a judgment of God upon the persecutors. He says, "When the Lord Jesus is revealed from heaven with his mighty angels in flaming fire," he will come with vengeance on those who do not know God. On that day the saints will be glorified in him, and the persecutors will suffer eternal punishment. In 1 Thessalonians 3:13, Paul again writes of the coming of our Lord Jesus with all his holy ones. Here he does not mention the coming in connection with judgment. It seems to be a quotation from Zechariah 14:5. In rabbinical literature the angels do not share in the final judgment as suggested in 2 Thessalonians, but in Jewish apocalyptic literature God is accompanied and assisted by angels.

In 1 Thessalonians the pressing questions of the community are related to what will happen to those who had die before Christ returns and when the event will occur. Will those who have died be raised? Or will the glorious age to come be reserved only for those who are alive at the coming of Christ? Paul calms their fears by affirming that the dead will rise first and "we who are alive . . . will be caught up together in the clouds together with them to meet the Lord in the air" (4:17). By using "we," Paul believed that he would be alive when this event took place. As to when the event would happen, Paul discarded any eschatological timetable and said, "The day of the Lord will come like a thief in the night" (5:2).

In his advice to the unmarried and widows in 1 Corinthians 7:25-31, Paul suggests that the unmarried refrain from marriage and the widows should not seek remarriage in view of the impending distress. The reason he gives is based on the constriction of time and the external form of this world passing away. Obviously, Paul believed in an immediate return of Christ and the termination of the age.

While Paul was carrying on a ministry in Ephesus, some representatives from the church in Corinth visited him and brought a letter from the congregation in which there were questions for Paul to answer. Along with this letter, the letters of Chloe, Stephanus, Fortunatus, and Achaicus told the apostle about some of the problems in the church. One of the problems was related to the teaching of the resurrection from the dead. It seems that some members of the congregation were convinced well enough that Jesus was raised from the dead, but they had doubts about their own resurrection. As Greeks, they were accustomed to immortality of the soul. When Paul appeared before the Areopagus in Athens and made his speech, what had not been clear to the Stoics and Epicureans previously when Paul preached in the agora had become very evident. In the agora they understood him to be introducing a new goddess (*anastasis*) with Jesus as the consort (Acts 17:18ff.). *Anastasis* means resurrection. When resurrection entered the picture, there were those who mocked Paul. The Stoics, influenced to some degree by Plato, believed that at the point of death the soul was absorbed into the world's soul.

In answering the skeptics in the church of Corinth, Paul set forth several clinching arguments. (1) If our hope is centered in this life alone, we are in a sad situation. (2) If we continue to use the symbol of baptism, it has no meaning because in this act we portray a death, burial and resurrection. (3) Paul used himself as an example and said "Why are we putting ourselves in danger every hour? I die every day! . . . If with merely human hopes I fought with wild animals at Ephesus, what would I have gained by it?" (1 Cor 15:30-32). (4) If there is no resurrection, we might as well live it up because "tomorrow we die."

In 1 Corinthians 15, after saying that all who are in Christ will be made alive (v. 22), the Apostle goes on to say that Christ was the first fruit, meaning that his resurrection was analogous to the sheaf of barley waved in the temple to commence the barley harvest ending with the wheat harvest in the Feast of Weeks. At the *Parousia* of Christ there will be a harvest of those who belong to Christ. They too will experience the resurrection. After this comes the end (*to telos*) when Christ will give over the rule to God. But before this occurs, Christ will have destroyed the evil powers dominating the present age. Paul adds, "The last enemy to be destroyed is death" (v. 26).

Just as he said in 1 Thessalonians, the Apostle reiterates here his assurance of being in the company of those who will be alive when Christ returns (vv. 51-54). He and others who are alive when this event happens will undergo a change from a physical body to a spiritual body. We observe that he used the trumpet (*shofar*) here as he did in 1 Thessalonians. Many of the apocalyptic writers used the blast of the trumpet to indicate the end of this age. In some cases it is Michael, the archangel, who blows the trumpet.

Paul sets up an imaginary objector to the resurrection who wants to know what kind of body those raised will have. In the various apocalyptic writings the resurrection has a variety of meanings. At times it is thought of as a resurrection of the righteous only. In Daniel it is a resurrection of the extremely good and the extremely bad. Sometimes the resurrection includes all. At times it is a resurrection to life on earth with a physical body. At other times it is a resurrection with a transformed body to life on a new earth. Sometimes we notice a resurrection to a life of spiritual bliss in heaven.

Many of the Jews believed in the resurrection of a crass materialistic body. They could not think of the preservation of one's personality by other means. The Greeks believed in immortality of the soul. If they followed Stoic thought, the person was absorbed into the world soul and thus lost his or her personality. *Logos* (Reason) had disseminated himself in the world of nature and individuals. At death the spark of divinity in each person went back to *Logos* (the world soul). Survival in this sense meant that *Logos* was getting himself back together.

Paul holds on to the personality of the individual by saying that one was raised in a body. Yet he avoids the crass materialistic view of a body and makes the resurrection a spiritual matter. Hence, Paul holds a view in between that of some Jews and Greeks. He presents several analogies to support his argument that one is raised in a spiritual body. In the Apocalypse of Baruch, written some forty years after Paul wrote to the church in Corinth, the writer says that the righteous dead will be raised in a physical body for two reasons: (1) to establish with certainty the identity of the person (50:2ff.). And (2) to show those raised that there was indeed a resurrection of the body. Later the physical body will be transformed so that those who are raised will look like angels (51:5).

In Paul's fourth letter to the Corinthians (2 Cor 1–9) we discover that the Apostle has come to the conclusion that he will not be alive at the *Parousia*. We say fourth letter because, in 1 Corinthians 5:9, Paul refers to a previous letter he had written to the church in Corinth. Thus, 1 Corinthians is a second letter. The third letter is found in 2 Corinthians 10–13, but is merely a fragment. The fourth letter is in chapters 1–9. Three of the letters were written from Ephesus, and the fourth was written from somewhere in the province of Macedonia.

At the beginning of his fourth letter (2 Cor 1:8), Paul reminds his readers of the grave nature of his recent affliction in the province of Asia (presumably while in Ephesus). The danger was so great that his life was at stake. The official sentence of death was pronounced upon him. What was this recent peril to which Paul alludes? In Acts 19:23-41, Luke tells of a riot in Ephesus instigated by Demetrius and a guild of silversmiths, but there is no suggestion that Paul's life was in danger. Two of his travel companions, Gaius and Aristarchus, were dragged into the theater; but the town clerk dismissed the charges brought against them. It is conceivable that at a later time Roman officials convened a court to hear a renewal of the charges against Paul and his companions. Luke does not mention any further trouble in Ephesus, but says that after the uproar Paul left for Macedonia. Of course, we are acutely aware that Luke omitted many events in the life of Paul that the Apostle himself relates in his epistles.

Was the affliction that crushed Paul a type of illness so terrific in nature that he actually despaired of life? We know that he had some constantly recurring ailment to which he referred in the third letter as a thorn in the flesh (2 Cor 12:7). We can hardly assume a reference to

75

illness here because the word used by Paul in verse 8 is *thlipsis*, and this is not the usual Greek word for illness. Furthermore, the sentence of death was definitely a judicial decision.

On the basis of certain passages in Paul's epistles, many scholars believe that the Apostle was in prison in Ephesus (Rom 16:7; 1 Cor 15:32; Phil 1:12-30; 2 Cor 6:5; 11:23). The argument is very convincing and deserves careful consideration. At any rate, we know that something happened to the Apostle in Ephesus far more severe than in the Demetrius riot mentioned by Luke. Whatever the situation, Paul did not go into the details because his readers apparently knew about it. In the midst of the crisis in Ephesus, Paul trusted in God and emerged safely from danger. Nevertheless, this incident caused him to reconsider his belief that he would be alive when Christ returned. Recent events in Ephesus and Macedonia and also the delay in Christ's coming lessened his degree of certainty of being present in the flesh at the end of time.

In light of the above, the Apostle realized that he must give consideration to a matter unmentioned in his previous letters. The question on his mind centered around the kind of existence a person had in the interim period between death and the end of the age. Before, when he faced questions from his converts about the resurrection, this problem had not been acute. Now he must consider the nature of existence in the interim between death and the resurrection. Paul never doubted that he would receive a spiritual body (2 Cor 5:1), but he seemed to say that if he died before Christ came, he must await the resurrection of the body until that event. Without a body he felt there was no possibility to express his personality. The experience meant a temporary loss of identity. He would be naked (2 Cor 5:3). Paul preferred to be present at Christ's coming and receive his spiritual body while he still possessed the physical body that the "mortal may be swallowed up by life" (v. 4).

While a majority of New Testament scholars are in general agreement with the previous interpretation given above, there are those who disagree. Some commentators press the literal sense of the present tense in the verb "have" in verse 1 and understand Paul to say that the

Christian is transformed into the resurrection body immediately upon death. Thus, the interval between death and the resurrection is ruled out, and there is no time for a disembodied spirit. This interpretation does not take into consideration what Paul had said previously in 1 Corinthians 15:23.

A few scholars maintain that the "building" (v. 1) provided by God is not a reference to the individual resurrection body but to the body of Christ. Since the Apostle used the metaphor "body of Christ" frequently to describe the relationship of all believers with Christ and with each other, they suppose Paul was asserting the same idea here. Our incorporation with Christ and sharing his personality in this life cannot be destroyed by physical death. They continue after death and are eternal. This view has much in its favor, even providing an answer to Paul's fear of disembodiment, but it is in conflict with verse 2. In this verse the apostle speaks about individual resurrection and not a corporate relationship in the body of Christ.

Though Paul shrank from the thought of dying before the *Parousia* and dreaded an existence without a body, he was still courageous (v. 6). He knew that during the interim period he would not be isolated from the presence of Christ. The indwelling Spirit was a pledge that this relationship with Christ could not be severed even temporarily in an intermediate state of existence but would be fuller and better.

Verse 10 of chapter 5 might lead one to think that Paul was not consistent in his theology by adhering to a teaching of salvation by works. Such an accusation is not justified, for he always upheld the principle of faith. Along with the Apostle's insistence that a person come into a right relationship with God by faith alone and his insistence that the directing power in the community of believers was in the Spirit, he firmly retained and stressed the belief that all persons, including believers, had to be judged by what they had done individually (1 Cor 4:4-5; Rom 2:6-11).

The prison epistles of Paul (Colossians, Philippians, Ephesians, and Philemon) contain nothing that is characteristic of apocalyptic except the forces of evil in the world. In Philippians he states,

We are expecting a Savior, the Lord Jesus Christ. He will transform
the body . . . that it may be conformed to the body of his glory, by
the power that also enables him to make all things subject to
himself. (3:20-21)

Nevertheless, he does not indicate an immediate return. The tradi-
tional view places these prison epistles in Rome. If this is true, the
Apostle, at the end of his career, moved away from his previous pattern of expressing things along apocalyptic lines. Even if the epistles
were written from Ephesus, and there is good evidence to support this
view, we are still nearing the end of Paul's missionary activity. The
epistles remaining would be Romans and 2 Corinthians 1–9, a letter
we have already examined.

Romans is one of the last epistles Paul wrote. This letter was written to a Christian community the Apostle did not establish. His hopes
were set on going to Rome, and, to prepare the way for his visit, he
wrote to the congregation in order to explain his theological position.
In chapters 9–11, a section unrelated to chapter 8 that precedes and
chapter 12 that follows, Paul expresses a deep concern for his fellow
Jews because they had not come into the faith as he had. After showing that God had not rejected Israel, but rather that Israel had rejected
God for lack of faith, in chapter 11, Paul interprets Israel's failure to
believe in Christ as causing the gospel to be preached to the Gentiles
with the intention of making the Jews jealous (v. 11). The hardening
of the heart on the part of Jews is evident in the present, but after a
sufficient number of the Gentiles believed, all Israel would be saved
(vv. 25-26). Though Paul does not mention the *Parousia* in this context, it is clear that he was not as sure now about the immediate
advent of Christ as he was in 1 Corinthians and the Thessalonian correspondence. He gives an extension of time for the gospel to be
proclaimed and accepted by the Gentiles and for the Jews also to
believe before the final consummation of all things.

Alongside his belief in an immediate *Parousia* of Christ, the
Apostle perceived that Christ was involved in our present human

situation to give life meaning. Like the author of the Gospel of John, he knew that Christ did not leave us orphans, but comes to us in the present. He was in Christ, and Christ was in him. At the end of the eighteenth century, Adolf Deissmann pointed out that the phrase *en Christo* (in Christ) or its equivalent occurred 164 times in Paul's epistles. Even if the Pastorals, 2 Thessalonians, and Ephesians are excluded the number is 117. This is a considerable number of times the union with Christ is mentioned. The *en christo* formula is something far removed from the ecstasies of the mystics. He has in mind a new life in a new context. In Christ we are a new creation. There is nothing vague or mysterious about his mysticism in which we try by our actions to get the attention of God, but rather a reacting mysticism whereby God acts to get our attention so that we respond by faith. Thus Paul lives in a tension between the Christ who is in us and the Christ who is to come at the consummation of the age.

We have already referred to two other influences of the apocalyptic on Paul. One was the allegory of Sarah and Hagar. There the Apostle mentions "the Jerusalem above" (Gal 4:26). The other is in 2 Corinthians 12:3-4 where Paul says that he was caught up into Paradise in the third heaven.

Though the Apostle shows that he was influenced by apocalyptic teachings, he does not launch out into endless speculations, grotesque imagery, and bizarre descriptions that are characteristic of this mind set. Interestingly, he does not mention any millenarian idea.

The Other Epistles

Jude, 2 Peter, and Hebrews are the only other epistles in the New Testament that contain an abundance of apocalyptic traits. Jude, written at the end of the first century or the early part of the second century A.D., is completely concerned with judgment. The twenty-five verses are saturated with Jewish apocalyptic literature. The author looks upon these writings as products equivalent to those of the Old

Testament and just as binding on Christians. We detect in verses 14b and 15 a direct quotation from 1 Enoch 1:9; in verse 13 the "wandering stars" is taken from 1 Enoch 18:15; and in verse 6, "the angels who did not keep their own position but left their proper dwelling" comes from 1 Enoch 10:5, 6, 12, 13. In addition, Jude refers to an incident recorded in the Assumption of Moses (v. 9). Here he mentions the contention between the archangel Michael and the devil about the body of Moses.

The purpose of Jude is to warn against false teachers who had entered the Christian community. He never tells what the teachings of these heretics are, but he gives a vivid picture of their character. They are grumblers, malcontents, and loudmouthed boasters (v. 16). They are also immoral and reject authority. The author says that all of the false teachers will experience doom and judgment as did their spiritual prototypes—the disobedient Israelites in the desert, the cities of Sodom and Gomorrah, and the fallen angels.

Our first knowledge of Jude comes from Tertullian, the presbyter from Carthage in the latter part of the second century A.D. He accepted this epistle as part of the *New Instrumentum* (the New Testament) because 1 Enoch is quoted in it.[1] Tertullian was disturbed about 1 Enoch being left out of the Old Testament. Apparently he did not know, as Clement of Alexandria tells us later, that Jude also quotes from the Assumption of Moses. There were many who expressed doubts about Jude being included in the canon of the New Testament. Some because of unknown authorship rejected it, and other perhaps due to the contents.

The second chapter of 2 Peter contains some of the material found in Jude, and from this scholars conclude that Jude is a condensation of 2 Peter, or 2 Peter is an expansion of Jude. The majority of scholars accept the latter view. Like Jude, 2 Peter was questioned a long time before it was finally incorporated into the New Testament. Our first knowledge of the epistle comes from the Alexandrian fathers in the third century A.D.

Like Jude, the author of 2 Peter warns his readers against false teachers. But more important, the writer desires to undergird the faith of his readers in the return of Christ. Though the author does not quote from any apocalyptic writing as Jude did, his allusions to this type of literature show his familiarity with it. His chief interest is a concern about the return of Christ. In chapter 3 he deals with the matter in great detail.

The author of 2 Peter reminds the recipients of his letter that scorners will come in the last days and ridicule those who believe that Christ will return. They said, "Where is the promise of his coming?" (3:4). They chide the believers by calling to their attention that nothing has changed in creation for possibly two generations (3:4). To counter the argument of the scoffers, the author awakens their memories relative to the destruction of the world by water in the time of Noah. This deluge came by the word of God, and "by the same word the present heavens and earth have been reserved for fire, being kept until the day of judgment and destruction of the godless" (3:7). In all the New Testament the only reference to the destruction of the world by fire is found in the epistle to Jude.

In Jewish apocalyptic writings the destruction of the world by water is mentioned a number of times, but more frequently they mention the coming judgment by fire. Did the author of 2 Peter get this notion from the apocalyptists or the Stoics? His source might spring from apocalyptic literature, for he shows acquaintance with the writings. Nevertheless, it appears more likely that his source is Stoic philosophy. The Stoics held that the universe was periodically destroyed by fire, and a new beginning came into existence. They used the expression *ekpurosis*, which meant a conflagration of the world by fire. The dissolving of the earth and the heavens and the elements melting with fire are expressions that tend to move in the direction of Stoic thought.

To the scorners who laugh at those who believe in the return of Christ, there comes an immediate reply from the author that God calculates time differently from human beings. He cites Psalm 90:4 as the way God measures time. "For a thousand years in your sight are like yesterday." He goes on to say that what appears to be slowness relative to God's promises is due to God's patience and forbearance. God does not desire that any should perish and wants them all to repent. Thus the delay of the day of the Lord is to give more people an opportunity to repent and believe.

Second Peter holds to the tradition in the synoptic Gospels and Paul in 2 Thessalonians that the day of the Lord will come like a thief in the night (3:10). The heavens and the earth will be consumed by fire, and new heavens and a new earth will be ushered in. Apparently, the author accepts the teaching of the Jewish apocalyptists concerning the creation of new heavens and a new earth and not a transformation of the universe as proclaimed by Isaiah 65:17 and 66:22.

Through the years, various names have been connected to the author of the epistle to the Hebrews. In the latter part of the second century A.D., Tertullian rejected the document because he believed Barnabas wrote it. In the third century, Clement of Alexandria attributed it to Paul. Origen of the same century knew of a tradition that associated the epistle with Clement of Rome. Other persons suggested as the author include Apollos; Priscilla, the wife of Aquila (both friends of Paul; the school of Stephen; Luke; Silvanus; and Philip. As to authorship, we go along with Origen who said, "Who wrote the epistle, the truth God knows."

Nearly all of the apocalyptic elements in Hebrews center around the heavenly city of Jerusalem that is to be in the future. Most of these traits are found in chapter 12. In 12:18-29, the author contrasts the old covenant made with Israel on Mount Sinai with the new covenant effected in Christ and says, "You have come to Mount Zion and to the city of the living God, the heavenly Jerusalem, and to innumerable angels in festal gathering" (v. 22). When the present visible world that is already waxing old is removed, the kingdom that cannot be shaken will remain (vv. 26-28). In the roll call of the faithful of the past in chapter 11, the writer says, "They desire a better country, that is, a heavenly one. Therefore, God is not ashamed to be called their God; indeed he has prepared a city for them" (v.16).

In the concluding chapter 13, the composer of the epistle exhorts his readers to join with Christ who was crucified outside the city's walls and to bear the reproach and stigma of the scandal of his crucifixion with him. He goes on to say, "For here we have no lasting city, but we are looking for the city that is to come" (v.14). As to the return of Christ, he is the only writer in the New Testament to use the word "second" in connection with the appearance of Christ. Other writers use a revelation of Jesus, the *parousia*, or a manifestation. In 10:25, the author refers to the Day as drawing near. The Day is the day of judgment of the wicked and presumably alludes to the appearance of Christ the second time.

There is nothing in 1 Peter, the epistles of John and James to indicate traces of Jewish apocalyptic borrowing on the part of the writers except that the time of judgment is near. There is nothing in the Pastorals except what is found in 1 Timothy 4:1-5. Here it is believed that in the later times there will be those who will apostatize and listen to evil spirits and teachings of demons (4:1).

Having examined the apocalyptic traits in the Gospels and Acts, Paul's epistles, and other epistles, we now take our leave and move into the apocalyptic fantasies of the book of Revelation.

Note

[1] Tertullian, *On Women's Dress* 1.2.3.

Chapter 6

THE BOOK OF REVELATION

The Gospels, Acts, and the Epistles were more sane and restrained in the use of apocalyptic features, but the author of Revelation went "full steam ahead" with the fuel he garnered from these writings. The book of Revelation portrays a closer resemblance to Jewish apocalyptic literature than any other book in the New Testament. Indeed, it is an apocalyptic writing *par excellence*. The ethical teachings of the gospel, the forte of Christianity, assume a subordinate role in this book. It has been said that Revelation lacks love, mercy, grace, and other Christian qualities, while it bears down on vengeance and destruction. True, it is far below the teachings of Jesus and the more enlightened portions of the Old Testament, but it is in full accord with the genre of literary works that revel in the destruction of enemies. Unless one is acquainted with this sort of writing, he or she might be forced to say that Revelation is sub-Christian.

The book of Revelation was not easily accepted into the canon of the New Testament. In the third century A.D., Dionysius, the bishop of Alexandria, raised some questions concerning the writing. From the fragments of his letters preserved by Eusebius we learn of his discussions about the book. Dionysius used evidence based on language, style, and contents to declare that Revelation could not stem from the author of the Fourth Gospel or 1 John. He admitted that some before him had discarded the book because they said that it was written by Cerinthus, the Gnostic, who forged the name of John to give credence to his own fabrications. He admitted that he was willing to allow the name John as author and that he had no doubt about its being inspired, but he said that the book could not have been written by the apostle John, the son of Zebedee. Though he did not reject Revelation, he did raise the question of its apostolicity. Thus, he implied that this book was not on the level with other books of the New Testament that had already gained recognition due to their apostolic nature. Some have suggested that he diminished the value of Revelation in order to curb the apocalyptic fervor and enthusiasm of the Egyptian monks.

Eusebius, the bishop of Caesarea, completed his *Ecclesiastical History* about A.D. 325. In his history he gives a list of New Testament books in four categories: (1) the acknowledged books, (2) the disputed books, (3) the spurious books, and (4) the rejected books (3.25). Among the acknowledged books he includes Revelation with the parenthetical statement (if it seems appropriate). In the spurious books he places Revelation with the same parenthetical statement. Apparently he was not certain how to classify this book. Eusebius was no critical scholar like Dionysius but gave the listings as to the number of churches that used them.

Athanasius, the bishop of Alexandria, gave a catalogue of the Old Testament and New Testament books in his Festal Epistle of A.D. 367, a letter to all Christendom announcing when Easter was to be observed. He removed any doubt about some of the Catholic epistles as well as Revelation by including them without question. Had there been new evidence that Athanasius received to remove those doubts? In the period between A.D. 325 and 367 we know of no such evidence. Could it be that Athanasius took advantage of his authority as bishop of Alexandria (so given since the time of Constantine) to declare when Easter was to be observed by also including all twenty-seven books of the New Testament, without any doubts, in order to deliver a blow at his arch enemy, Eusebius of Caesarea, who wavered on some of the Catholic epistles and Revelation? Though this might seem unlikely, we must bear in mind that Athanasius hated Eusebius with a passion. It could be that during one of his banishments from Egypt while he was in Rome, Athanasius compared the opinions on the canon of the Eastern churches with that of the Western churches, and some sort of common agreement was reached with the religious leaders of Rome. Heretofore, Revelation had been accepted by the Western churches.

Cyril, bishop of Jerusalem; Gregory of Nazianzus, bishop of Constantinople; Amphilochius, bishop of Iconium; John Chrysostom, bishop of Constantinople; and Theodore, bishop of Mopsuestia, were all religious leaders who were contemporaries of Athanasius, and they omitted the book of Revelation. Furthermore, the translation of the Greek text of the New Testament into Syriac by Rabbula, the bishop of Edessa, in the fifth century A.D., does not include Revelation and some of the Catholic epistles. On the basis of the testimony of the above religious leaders, we must conclude that the bishops of other Eastern churches did not hold to the opinion of Athanasius.

Martin Luther, the reformer of the sixteenth century, did not have much use for the book of Revelation. In 1522, he said that this writing was neither prophetic nor apostolic. In his 1522 German translation of the New Testament from the Greek, he gave numbers to the twenty-seven New Testament books. There were twenty-three numbers followed by a space, and then he listed Hebrews, James, Jude, and Revelation without any serial numbers. This is no indication he put these books out of the canon, but it does show that he considered these four books of lesser value. In his 1534 German translation of the New Testament, though he still considered Revelation to be a dumb prophecy, he left it up to the individual reader to determine its value. He admitted the book could be used for consolation and warning to Christians.

John Calvin, the Swiss reformer who was a contemporary of Luther, wrote a commentary on every book of the New Testament with the exception of 2 and 3 John and Revelation. He occasionally quoted from Revelation, but those citations say nothing about his view of the book. Why did he not comment on Revelation, a book that had been disputed in the Eastern churches? Calvin quoted from Eusebius frequently, so that we know he was acquainted with Eusebius' vacillation concerning the document. Ulrich Zwingli, a Swiss reformer who was a contemporary of Calvin, thought that Revelation should be excluded from the Bible.

Now that we have seen the clouds of doubt engulfing the book of Revelation and the unwillingness of some to include it in the canon of the New Testament, let us deal with the matter of authorship. The author simply identified himself as John. But the question is: Which John? Was it John, the apostle who was the brother of James and the son of Zebedee? Tradition says it was this John, but tradition also denies he was the author.

About the middle of the second century A.D., Papias, bishop of Hierapolis, mentioned that there were two Johns who lived in Ephesus. One was John, the son of Zebedee, and the other was John the elder. The way Eusebius quotes the saying of Papias leads us to believe that John the elder came after the time of John the apostle. However, Papias says nothing about John the apostle writing anything. Some time after A.D. 150, Justin Martyr, who at one time lived in Ephesus, declared that John the apostle was the author of Revelation.[1] We wonder whether Justin can be trusted because he gives some material that is apocryphal relative to the life of Jesus. Justin often refers to *Memoirs* or *Memoirs of the Apostle* but never to the Gospel of John.

Irenaeus, the bishop of Lyons in Gaul, in his early life resided in Smyrna, a city north of Ephesus. He said that all of the Johannine writings were by a single author, but his identification of the person is so vague that his meaning cannot be firmly established. It is widely accepted that John the apostle is meant. However, out of forty-seven occurrences of the name John, he gave him the title of apostle only twice. Sixteen times he called John a disciple of the Lord. We notice in the Papias tradition that the title disciple was applied to John the elder. It is interesting to note that Ignatius, the bishop of Antioch, in his letter to the church in Ephesus about A.D. 115, says much about Paul, but he does not mention John the apostle. Surely if John had lived in Ephesus, he would have made some remark about him.

Tertullian, a presbyter from Carthage, in his later years was influenced by Montanism. The New Prophecy, as it was called, was initiated by Montanus, a pagan priest of the province of Phrygia in Asia Minor. Montanus was converted to Christianity and started a movement that spread like a wildfire through Asia Minor, along North Africa, and finally into Spain and Gaul. He was greatly influenced by the book of Revelation and the Gospel of John. He promoted millenarian teachings and was deeply concerned about the immediate return of Christ. Tertullian was captivated by the concepts of Montanus, and in his book *Against Marcion* he described the heavenly city, the New Jerusalem, which was seen by unbelievers in Judea suspended in the sky for forty days.

In the second century an attack was launched against the Montanists in Asia Minor. In the early part of the third century a similar reaction occurred in Rome. In Asia Minor, the opponents were labeled *Alogi* by Ephipanius, the bishop of Constantia (Salamis) in A.D. 375. Previous to that time they had not been given a name. A decade or two after the *Alogi* appeared in Asia Minor, the Roman presbyter Gaius adopted their position.

In response to the Montanists who considered their leader as the *Paraclete* (John 14:26) and anticipated the imminent descent of the New Jerusalem in Phrygia, the *Alogoi* contended that the Gospel of John and the book of Revelation were written by the Jewish Christian heretic Cerinthus. The reaction to the Gospel of John and Revelation does not seem to have been an organized endeavor but rather the opinion of a group of Christians who knew that something was wrong with the interpretation of the Montanists and Gnostics; yet, they knew no other means to counter their arguments other than to reject the documents. Notably, the *Alogoi* were never classified as heretics. They remained in the church because at that period of time criticism of the documents was tolerated as long as one opposed the heretics with the most drastic measures.

Church tradition, some of which might be well established and some less reliable, affirms that John the apostle went to Asia Minor after the destruction of Jerusalem and performed a pastoral ministry in the province of Asia including Ephesus. One tradition says he was thrown into boiling oil at Rome but was unharmed. Still, another tells of John being banished to the Isle of Patmos. Legends embellishing the latter days of John report that he drank poison and did not die, raised the dead, converted a notorious robber, refused to be caught with the heretic Cerinthus in a public bath in Ephesus, and was carried to worship services during his feeble years. Another tradition, which would nullify all the stories given above, tells us that John suffered early martyrdom along with his brother James.

It is impossible for us to present a character analysis of any of the disciples of Jesus. Any attempt is impracticable and absurd because the authors of the Gospels were primarily interested in the person, words and works of Jesus. Occasionally, we do encounter some comments made by the Twelve that might reveal their innermost thoughts and feelings. In three different stories recorded by the synoptic gospels, John (in two of these James his brother is with him) becomes the center of attention due to his peculiar views concerning the mission of Jesus.

The first story portrays John the apostle as bigoted and intolerant. John had met an exorcist who was using the name of Jesus as a formula to cast out demons. The exorcist was willing to identify himself with Jesus and the company of disciples. John was so displeased with the man that he reprimanded him and told him to stop using the name of Jesus in his exorcisms (Mark 9:38: Luke 9:49). Jesus was surprised by John's attitude of intolerance and rebuked him with a reminder that as long as the exorcist did not speak evil of him he should be treated as an ally and not as an enemy.

The second glimpse into the character of John comes solely from Luke's Gospel. Luke has a special section in his Gospel beginning at 9:51 and continuing through 18:14. It is commonly called Luke's Travel Narrative. At the beginning of the travel narrative Jesus with his disciples was journeying through the territory of the Samaritans. He sent some of his followers ahead to make arrangements for his lodging in a village. The inhabitants of the village refused Jesus and his disciples hospitality because they were Jews and because they were headed toward Jerusalem. The refusal of hospitality by the Samaritans prompted John and James to fight back. They wanted Jesus to call down fire from heaven and consume their hateful enemies. Jesus could not condone this spirit of vindictiveness and rebuked the "sons of thunder."

The third revelation into the mind set of John comes from Mark 10:35-45. Here the self-interest of John comes before us very vividly. He and his brother James sought positions of honor in what they thought was to be a political kingdom established by Jesus. They wanted to outrank the other disciples. They were status seekers. Jesus calmly reminded the sons of Zebedee that in his service there was no place for the pagan concept that stressed the exercise of authority. True greatness carried with it the readiness to be a slave to all.

In the early portions of Acts, John in the company of Simon Peter plays an important role in the early church. He and Peter bore their testimony about the risen Lord in the temple area (3:1). They were both arrested by the religious authorities, imprisoned, arraigned before the council, and charged not to preach again in the name of Jesus. John and Peter were appointed by the church in Jerusalem to investigate the work of Philip among the Samaritans. They endorsed the admission of these people into the fellowship because they, too, received the Holy Spirit. What a change in attitude by John over his previous encounter with the Samaritans when he wanted to call down fire from heaven and consume them! The apostle Paul tells us that on one of his trips to Jerusalem he saw John, James (the brother of Jesus), and Peter. He referred to these as three "pillars" of the church (Gal 2:9). So far as we know from the New Testament, John continued his ministry in Jerusalem witnessing to the Jews and working with Jewish Christians without showing the slightest desire to proclaim the gospel to the Gentiles.

In the light of what we know about John the apostle from the Gospels, it is easy to see how his name could be associated with Revelation. The vindictive and bigoted attitude of John is so evident from the Gospels, yet we detect a change of perspective in Acts. The attitude of the author of Revelation with his "hellfire and brimstone" message seems to fit the picture of John in the Gospels. Prejudice, if deep-rooted, is hard to remove from a person. On the other hand, the conflicting traditions about John the apostle make it difficult for us to believe that he was the author of Revelation.

The book of Revelation, contrary to almost all other apocalyptic writings, supposedly is not pseudonymous. Could it be that the writer did not depart from the regular apocalyptic procedure of taking a name of a worthy of the past? If so, what worthy of the past would it be? Dare we suggest John the Baptist? Josephus, the Jewish historian, extolled John the Baptist and said the people were moved by his words. In fact, Herod Antipas was so afraid of the great influence John had over the people, he decided to put him to death. Herod Antipas was alarmed because he thought John might stir the people to rebel.

When Herod was defeated by Aretas IV, king of the Nabateans, many Jews contended that the defeat was due to having John the Baptist killed.

In Matthew and Luke we notice that the preaching of John the Baptist is very much akin to apocalyptic eschatology (Matt 3:10, 12; Luke 3:9, 17). Matthew and Luke also record the coming of John's disciples to ask in the name of John if Jesus was the "one who is to come" or if he should look for another (Matt 11:2ff; Luke 7:18ff.). Jesus' reply was to tell John what he was doing and that he must not take offense by what he did. Jesus invited John to answer his own question. No doubt John thought that Jesus was doing those things incoherent with his understanding of his function. John had preached judgment, but Jesus was just healing people. The watchword of the Baptist was from Isaiah 40:3, which incidentally was the watchword of the Qumran community. Some scholars maintain that John was a member of the Essenic group before he launched out on his own. If this is true, he would have been obsessed with apocalyptic notions of this community. We have previously noted from Josephus and documents safeguarded by this community that the apocalyptic elements mixed with militarism were very strong.

The John the Baptist sect was very influential in the first century A.D. In the Gospels and Acts we detect apologetic undertones indicating a conflict between the disciples of Jesus and the disciples of John. We also notice the emphasis on the inferiority of John to Jesus. Even today the Baptist sect exists in Iraq under the name of the Mandeans.

When Paul made a second visit to Ephesus, he found twelve disciples of John the Baptist. Those disciples had not heard of the Holy Spirit but had only been baptized into John's baptism (Acts 19:2ff.). The Apostle baptized them into the name of the Lord Jesus, and they received the Holy Spirit. Previous to Paul's arrival in Ephesus, Aquila and Priscilla had confronted a similar situation in the case of Apollos, the Alexandrian Jew. Apollos had been instructed "in the way of the Lord" and spoke accurately about the things concerning Jesus but was only acquainted with John's baptism. Aquila and Priscilla expounded to him "the way of God" more accurately.

The two incidents above clearly show the influence of the disciples of John the Baptist in Ephesus, one of the cities to which the author of Revelation wrote. Adding to the influence of the Baptist in Ephesus the inconclusiveness of the traditions placing a ministry of the apostle John in Ephesus, it is quite conceivable that a person assumed the name of John the Baptist and wrote the book of Revelation. There is no doubt that the author was a Jewish Christian, and presumably he could have readily accepted apocalyptic ideas from his Jewish heritage. It is noteworthy that John the Baptist in the Fourth Gospel calls Jesus "the Lamb of God, who takes away the sin of the world" (1:29). In Revelation the author refers to the risen Christ as Lamb twenty-seven times. In the Fourth Gospel the word for Lamb is amnos, whereas in Revelation *arnion* is used.

The author of Revelation begins by claiming to have received a revelation of Jesus Christ through an angel concerning what was to occur soon. The message is urgent and must be read aloud before Christians who are to keep what is written. John said he was on the Isle of Patmos when he had the vision. What was he doing on the Isle of Patmos? Was he a prisoner? Was he a missionary? Traditionally, interpreters have assumed he was a prisoner because he said that he was on the island "because of the word of God and the witness of Jesus" (1:9). Yet this phrase does not say specifically that he was a prisoner. His vision was to be shared with the seven churches of the Roman province of Asia in Asia Minor. Why did the author omit Hierapolis, Colossae, Troas, Tralles, and Magnesia? All of these were also in the province of Asia.

In his vision John saw the triumphant Christ who could not be defeated by official Judaism, the Roman emperor, or any other evil force in the future. Much of what he saw was based on descriptive terms that came from Daniel, Ezekiel, and Isaiah. Like other visionaries, he told what was at hand, and he had little interest in the far distant future. It is not until we come to chapters 20–22 that we have anything similar to the prediction of the end time, and even then he dresses this up in ideas already set forth in other apocalyptic works. In six instances the writer tells the churches what was to occur immediately (1:1, 3; 22:7, 10, 12, 20). After announcing six times about what he expected to happen soon, we should take him at his word. The future he had in mind was then.

To explain his vision, the Seer of Patmos draws from a variety of sources. From the Old Testament he cites sections from Daniel, Ezekiel, Isaiah, Zechariah, Exodus, Joel, and the Psalms. As a matter of fact, most of the Seer's vision is a revamping of Ezekiel. In addition to the above sources, he copied from current apocalyptic literary works, mythology, and the oracle of impending doom on Jerusalem recorded in Mark 13.

To understand Revelation, one must realize that the teachings were conditioned by persecution and martyrdom. The keynotes are faith, courage, witness, and endurance. In his letters to the churches John shows a deep concern for some members of the congregations who were led astray by heresy. He believed that persecution could not impede the advance of Christianity but heresy might. Therefore, he called upon his readers to take a firm stand against teachings that were not consistent with the Christian faith, so that they may be prepared for the coming persecution.

It is clear that the Seer wrote down his vision first (chaps. 4–22) and then composed the letters to the seven churches of Asia. To the church in Ephesus he promised that those who conquered would eat of the tree of life in the paradise of God (22:2, 14). Those who conquered in Smyrna would be exempt from the second death (20:6). The conquerors in the church of Pergamum could partake of the hidden manna and receive a white stone (19:12). To the victors of Thyatira the morning star was promised (22:16). The faithful in Sardis would be included in the book of life (20:12; 21:27). To those who endured in Philadelphia was given the promise,

> I will make you a pillar in the temple of my God. . . . I will write on you the name of my God, and the name of the city of my God, the new Jerusalem that comes down from my God out of heaven, and my own new name. (3:12)

Unfortunately there is nothing in the vision proper equivalent to what is given in the letter to the church of Laodicea.

John gives us enough information about the seven churches to let us know that Christians were involved in a bitter struggle against the pagan society in which they lived. They were surrounded by religions of all sorts. There were mystery cults, astral religion, Roman emperor worship, the Olympian deities, the worship of Asclepius (the Greek god of medicine) syncretistic religions galore, the worship of Artemis, and philosophies. Since the Christians were few in number in these cities, it was extremely difficult for them to bear the brunt of the criticisms leveled against them for abstaining from the evil practices of the citizenry. It was much easier to compromise their Christian faith and go along with the majority. John knew that some of the Jews had already succumbed to the pressure and had gone the way of the Ophite cult. John said those Jews were of the Synagoue of Satan and though they claimed to be Jews, they were not. The Ophite cult worshiped the snake, and this is why he called it the Synagogue of Satan.

Were the letters actually sent to the seven churches? If so, did John make seven copies of the vision proper (chaps. 4–22)? Did each copy include all the letters to the churches? If this is true, then the author hangs out the dirty linen of each church for all to see. If he sent each church a separate letter along with the vision, it would seem that we would have manuscripts with separate letters, but we do not have them. It is possible that the Seer of Patmos chose seven churches of the province of Asia as representatives of different reactions to the pagan society, and the letters were merely a literary device. We have already mentioned that there were more churches in the province of Asia than just the seven.

Due to apocalyptic influence, the author liked to use the number seven. He has seven letters, seven lampstands, seven angels of presence, seven bowls, seven trumpets, seven seals, seven emperors, seven horns of the Lamb, seven spirits of God, seven stars, seven thunders, seven holy angels, seven beatitudes, half of seven years, seven-fold power, and seven classes of inhabitants of the earth. To add to John's use of seven from Jewish apocalyptic writings, there was Hellenistic mysticism replete with sevens. There were seven vowels, seven strings of the lyre, the seven spheres, seven heavens, seven colors, seven metals, and seven days of the week.

It is rather strange that the Seer did not mention the apostle Paul in the letter to Ephesus. Paul, Aquila, and Priscilla established a congregation in Ephesus. Paul spent nearly three years in the city proclaiming the gospel. In his last trip to Jerusalem, Paul met with the Ephesian elders at Miletus. He reviewed his ministry among the Ephesians and delivered some admonitions and warnings in his farewell address. About twenty years later Ignatius, the bishop of Antioch, was not so negligent. He made much of Paul in his letter to the Ephesians.

The Vision

John's vision, which he was commanded to share with the seven churches, begins in chapter 4. Like Enoch, he was caught up into heaven and saw what he customarily saw in the temple in Jerusalem. Around the throne of God were twenty-four courses of priests, the four living creatures representing the doubling of the cherubim in Solomon's temple just as Ezekiel did, and other fixtures in the temple relating to worship. In the heavenly sphere the author observed complete harmony and accord; but with the opening of the seven seals, the blowing of the shofars, and the pouring out of the bowls of wrath, discordant notes on the earth filled the air.

Along with the awe-inspiring sense of worship in his vision, John saw Christ as a Lamb appearing to have been slain. The Lamb was standing. The author used the Greek word *hestekos*, a perfect participle, carrying the meaning of completed action and a continuance of the action. Did he wish to convey the idea that "standing" was equivalent to the Jewish *Tamid*? The *Tamid* was the continual burnt offering in the temple. This ritual was performed in the morning and evening every day of the year. One of the tractates in the Mishnah is devoted to a description of this offering, and it receives the title *Tamid*.

Instead of viewing Christ as the crucified one, does he use the analogy of the *Tamid* to express the same thought? In the daily sacrifice the sacrificial lamb was killed, the blood was collected, and the parts of the lamb were placed on the altar to be burned. In one portion of the ceremony some of the blood was poured at the base of the altar. Other New Testament writers used different analogies.

According to the Fourth Gospel, Jesus was crucified on the day the Passover lamb was killed, which was the fourteenth day of Nisan. The synoptic Gospels agree on the fifteenth day of Nisan, the day after the Passover lamb was killed. It seems that the Fourth Gospel is attempting to show that Jesus was crucified as our Passover. On one occasion, the apostle Paul used the analogy of the Passover. He said, "For our paschal lamb, Christ, has been sacrificed" (1 Cor 5:7b). On another occasion, Paul compared Christ's death to an action taken by the high priest on the Day of Atonement. On this day the high priest went into the Holy of Holies, and at the mercy seat he received a revelation from God once each year. He came out of the Holy of Holies and shared the revelation with the people. Paul, on the other hand, said that Christ is our mercy seat; and, contrary to the secret manner in which only the high priest knew the revelation from God, Christ is put forward as the mercy seat, not enclosed in a Holy of Holies privately, but for all to see for themselves the revelation of God.

In the Epistle to the Hebrews, the death of Christ is presented as a sacrifice connected with *Yom Kippur* (the Day of Atonement). Christ is not only high priest after the order of Melchizedek, but is the offering for the sacrifice as well. However, his offering is a dedication to do the will of God. Since the author of the Fourth Gospel, Paul, and the author of the epistle to the Hebrews used sacrifices of the Jews as analogies relative to the death of Christ, there is the likelihood that the Seer of Patmos introduced the Jewish daily offering (*Tamid*) as an analogy.

In 1931, Philip Carrington presented numerous allusions to the Tamid in his study of Revelation.[2] He might have gone overboard in suggesting these allusions; nevertheless, we believe that John made some use of the daily sacrifice in the framework of his document. The daily sacrifice played an important role in the worship of the Jews. It symbolized Israel's pledge of unbroken service to God. The essentialness of the *Tamid* was stressed quite frequently in Jewish apocalyptic writings. The author of Daniel was distressed when Antiochus Epiphanes discontinued the daily sacrifice of the Jews (11:31; 12:11). For the sake of convenience, let us place side by side the order of the *Tamid* in the Mishnah and allusions in Revelation to that ritual.

Mishnah, Tamid	Revelation
1. The killing of the lamb	1. Christ is the lamb appearing to have been slain
2. Three blasts from the shofar and the opening of the gates of the temple	2. The seven shofars (8:1) and the opening of the temple in heaven (11:19)
3. Interval of prayer (the priests retire to the Chamber of Hewn Stone)	3. Interlude to retire for offering incense (8:1ff)
4. Offering of the incense	4. The smoke of incense (8:4)
5. Drink offering (wine is poured at the base of the altar); the residue of the blood of the lamb is poured at the base of the altar	5. The cry of the martyrs whose blood has been spilled at the base of the altar (6:6-9)
6. Every day of the week the Levites sang a new song	6. The new song (5:9; 14:3)
7. The pouring out of the drink offering was for reconciliation	7. The pouring out of the seven bowls of God's wrath for destruction (16:1ff.)
8. The burnt offering	8. Jerusalem is the burnt offering, and her smoke goes up forever and ever (18:8; 19:3)

As we compare the pattern in the *Tamid* and in Revelation, it is apparent that a similarity exists. Though the Seer did not follow the ritual of the daily sacrifice in the exact order, he gave enough of the details to show his familiarity with this religious observance. Some scholars see a great divergence between the three soundings of the shofar in the *Tamid* ritual and the seven soundings in Revelation. This is true, but the three blasts of the shofars come at the beginning of the ritual. However, there are many other soundings throughout the ceremony as recorded in the Mishnah. It just so happens that John liked to use the number seven.

In the right hand of God John saw a scroll written on the *recto* and *verso* sides of the papyrus roll. When the angel asked, "Who is worthy to open the scroll and break its seals?" (5:2), for a time it seemed that no one was worthy to do the job, and the Seer began to weep. One of the elders told him to stop his crying because the Lion of the tribe of Judah, the Root of David, had conquered and was able to break the seals. Suddenly, this Lion has become a Lamb for the daily sacrifice. Christ had come in humiliation by his death on the altar of sacrifice (equivalent to the crucifixion), but now he is a lion with power. He is the exalted Christ. The living creatures together with the twenty-four elders sing a new song depicting the humiliation and the glorification. Joining the creatures and the elders in the adoration of the Lamb are 10,000 upon 10,000 angels saying, "Worthy is the Lamb that was slaughtered, to receive power and wealth and wisdom and might and honor and glory and blessing" (5:12). This is followed by universal praise to God and the Lamb, indicating they are equal in greatness, power, and majesty.

The Seven Seals

Enoch, Jubilees, and the Testaments of the Twelve Patriarchs all refer to the "heavenly tablets" on which the secrets of the ages are recorded. In 1 Enoch it is stated that the "heavenly tablets" record "all the deeds of mankind . . . to the remotest generations" (81:2). These tables outline the whole history of the world (93:2) and in particular intro-duce the greater iniquities that will come on the earth (106:19). The heavenly tablets in Jewish apocalyptic writings bear a close resem-blance to the "tablets of destiny" in the scene in Revelation when the Lamb who was overcome is alone permitted to take the scroll from God and break the seals on the scroll.

Admittedly, the Jewish apocalyptic writers made use of the "heav-enly tablets" to predict the future as well as a history of the past, but we must also remember that much of what they predicted for the future had already happened when they wrote. This is the same course the Seer of Patmos takes. The secrets disclosed upon the opening of the various portions of the scroll that had been sealed have to do with something that has already happened in history. This is also true in the case of the sounding of the seven shofars and the pouring out of the seven bowls of wrath. The Seer of Patmos is presenting under the guise of predictions what has already occurred. In doing this he conforms to the pattern of the apocalyptists who preceded him.

The author of Revelation divides the seven seals, seven trumpets, and the seven bowls into two parts. The first section takes up four incidents, and the second section takes up the remaining three. Christ, the Lamb, tears off the first seal, and one of the living creatures issues the command, "go" or "come" (the Greek imperative *erchou* can mean either one). The first pictorial enactment is a rider on a white horse representing ambition and conquest. This rider is followed by a horse-man on a red horse showing what happens when an ambitious person desires to lead people into a bloody conflict. The result is war and bloodshed that robs the world of peace. The third rider is on a black horse to demonstrate what occurs when nations fight against nations. It produces a famine. The final rider sits upon a clorax horse (pale green). He brings death. These four events inevitably befall humanity when someone gets the notion to conquer other nations. There is a downward progression from ambition, to bloodshed, to famine, and then to death. This has been the course of history and will continue as such until people are willing to live in peace.

When the fifth seal is broken, John sees at the base of the altar those who gave their lives for the Word of God. Their death is compared to the daily sacrifice of the Jews. Their blood had been poured out at the base of the altar for sacrifice. Does the author include Christians in the group, or are they Jewish martyrs? If so, it is only by anticipation just as it is in chapter 7 in the sealing of the servants of God. Throughout the book John uses "the word of God" and "the testimony of Jesus" (1:2, 9; 12:17; 20:4) or the equivalent to include faithful Jews and Christians.

The martyrs cry out to God for vengeance upon those who caused their death. This is very unlike the cry of Christ from the cross, "Father forgive them; for they do not know what they are doing" (Luke 23:34) or the cry of Stephen when he was stoned, "Lord, do not hold this sin against them" (Acts 7:60). Nevertheless, the usual reaction in Jewish apocalyptic literature was similar to that of the martyrs in Revelation. When will God act and defend the people God has chosen? How long will godless imperialism continue? Why does God not intervene and destroy our enemies? Has God forsaken the people with whom God made a covenant? These and many more like questions came from the Jews who were killed by their enemies.

The breaking of the sixth seal ushers in a judgment of God as an answer to the prayers of the martyrs. What is presented is not to be taken literally. John is following the rhetorical exaggerations of the prophets in describing the Day of Yahweh. He also uses his poetic imagination just as the prophets did. The Seer might have in mind natural phenomena such as earthquakes, falling meteors, and eclipses. These would be signs to sinners that judgment is at hand. More than likely, the answer to the prayers of the martyrs is to be taken symbolically. Monarchs rise and fall. Militarists have their day and come to a fatal end. The rich and the strong feel secure, but their security turns into insecurity. There are social upheavals and political disasters. The author looks upon these troubles in the world as a judgment of God.

Before the Lamb breaks the seventh seal, "time out" is called to mark those who are exempt from judgment. John follows the symbolism of Ezekiel 9:4-6 where the faithful of Israel are sealed on the forehead to protect them from destruction when God punishes Jerusalem. John presents a different view, however. The four angels are restrained from the destruction of the earth and sea by another angel who calls for a delay until the faithful servants of God receive the mark on their foreheads. The author does not mean that they are to be protected from death, but they are sealed to indicate they are on God's side. These are martyrs, but they will have a privileged place in the resurrection. John also has in mind the destruction of Jerusalem that will come later.

Twelve thousand from each of the tribes of Israel (144,000 total), who have shown their faithfulness to the Word of God, are marked. Clearly, these are loyal Jews because we are still in the pre-Christian stage of history. We observe that the author omits Dan among the tribes. We can only assume this omission is due to the Testaments of the Twelve Patriarchs in which the tribe of Dan is controlled by Satan (Dan 5:6). The author also leaves out Ephraim, but he includes Manasseh. Both of these were Joseph tribes. Possibly he meant Ephraim when he listed the tribes of Joseph.

After the true Jews are sealed, John sees a great multitude that no one can count. They are clothed in white robes, and they introduce a new kind of song to the great liturgy of creation. Their chant is, "Salvation to our God who sits upon the throne, and to the Lamb." The angel tells John that the great multitude represents those who have come out of the great tribulation. Their robes are whitened by the blood of the Lamb. Though the author has not yet introduced us to Christianity, he, by anticipation, allows us to see the Gentiles who confess the name of Christ and become martyrs. Some have suggested that the scene of the great multitude of Gentiles was originally the climax of the book.

When the Lamb breaks the seventh seal, we expect something terrible to happen, but instead there is a period of silence for thirty minutes. In the ritual of the *Tamid*, this is the time for the priests to retire to the Chamber of the Hewn Stone and participate in the incense offering. In the ceremony a priest, selected by lot, stands at the altar with a golden censer and places coals of fire into the censer. He then puts incense on the top of the coals of fire. Smoke ascends in the temple representing the prayers of the people. Moses Maimonides,[3] a rabbi of the twelfth century A.D. and one of the great Jewish philosophers and theologians, in commenting on the daily sacrifice said that the incense offering acted as a deodorant to dispel the scent of the slaughtered animals.

According to the pattern of the *Tamid*, an angel takes the golden censer, and much incense is given to the angel to be mixed with the prayers of the saints. The rising smoke from the incense pot risees to heaven with the prayers of the saints. It is possible that the saints are those whose blood was poured out at the base of the altar. They are the ones who cried out for revenge on those who put them to death (see 6:10). The residue of coals left in the censer are thrown on the earth. This results in peals of thunder, voices, flashes of lightning, and an earthquake, all of which symbolize the power, majesty, and presence of God. There follows the blowing of the seven shofars in succession as an answer to the prayers of the saints.

The Seven Trumpets

Like the first four seals, the four shofars form a unit of their own. The convulsions of nature bring disaster and judgment upon those who are wicked. The catastrophes come upon the earth, sea, rivers, and sky. But judgment is only fractional. It covers only one-third of each element. It appears that the author is indicating that judgments in the past have been partial, and the full measure of God's judgment is yet to come. The four calamities are not to be taken literally. It seems that the author has in mind the destruction of Sodom and Gomorrah, the plagues of Egypt, and other devastations in the Old Testament associated with the judgment of God. In the first four seals judgment comes upon humanity by evil men, but now punishment comes from heaven. There seems to be no suggestion by John that the judgments in the four shofars, and the four bowls of wrath are progressive.

Rather, they are distributive from men, God, demons, and demon-possessed men.

Before the fifth angel blows his shofar, John sees an eagle in flight crying, "Woe, woe, woe to the inhabitants of the earth" (8:13). One of the fallen angels (perhaps Satan himself) opens the shaft of the bottomless pit, and a horde of locusts come out when the fifth angel blows the shofar. The swarm of locusts comes from the prophet Joel. Joel proclaimed that locusts would devastate the land, and this judgment, in the Day of Yahweh, would be succeeded by a swarm of soldiers, innumerable like the locusts, who would ravage the land (chaps. 1–2). In like fashion John sets forth two stages. When the fifth shofar is blown, the demons from the bottomless pit resembling locusts come forth to make mankind sin against God. The angel who sounds the sixth shofar brings in 200,000,000 demon-possessed men. Men inspired by the demonic bring a partial destruction upon humanity. Even then, some do not repent, nor give up worshiping demons or idols, nor cease from their immoral actions.

The fifth and sixth shofars indicate the two "woes" proclaimed by the eagle flying in midheaven, but there is one more "woe" to come. Before the author introduces the third "woe" (the seventh shofar), he pauses for an interlude. The interlude begins at 10:1 and goes to 11:13.

Prior to chapter 10, all that is mentioned by John has to do with the distant past, except for the anticipatory picture of the multitude of Gentile Christians in 6:9-12. Now he shifts to the more immediate past by letting us know of his call to be a prophet. As a prophet he is the harbinger of the inauguration of the Christian era. Could it be that this is another veiled intimation showing us that the author of Revelation takes the name of John the Baptist? John the Baptist was declared to be a prophet and the forerunner of Jesus.

The mighty angel told John that the blowing of the seventh angel on the shofar would usher in the mystery of God. It was to be fulfillment of the message of the prophets. The mystery of God, as we learn later, is the coming of Christ and the kingdom of God. The Seer himself is to have a role in the prophetic announcements. This does not make too much sense if he is already in the Christian era, unless in true apocalyptic form he presents the present as the past. Of course, if he takes the name of John the Baptist, the call of the seer to be a prophet fits very well for John the Baptist who was the precursor of Jesus.

The call of the Seer of Patmos is very similar to the call of Ezekiel. It appears that he copied the call of Ezekiel to be a prophet and made it his own claim to prophecy. There are only a few differences in the two accounts. In Ezekiel 2:8–3:3, it is God who gives the prophet the scroll to eat, whereas in Revelation an angel gives a little scroll to John for him to eat. The little scroll is in contrast to the scroll with the seven seals. When John ate the scroll, it was as sweet as honey in his mouth, just as in the case of Ezekiel, but when the papyrus scroll reached his stomach, there was a bitter taste. Ezekiel does not mention the bitterness of the scroll in his stomach, but John equates the words of lamentation, mourning, and woe with the bitterness of the prophetic role. Anyone who was called to fill the prophetic role felt indeed honored. It was a religious privilege many could covet. Yet the call carried with it the pronouncement of doom, which was a very unpopular message. The idealism of the selection to be a prophet waned with the responsibility of revealing the judgments of God on the people.

A second part of the interlude begins in chapter 11. The Seer is given a measuring rod to measure the temple of God, the altar, and those who worship in the temple. Here again the author goes back to Ezekiel who is called upon to measure the temple and the temple area (Ezek 40–46). The vision of Ezekiel was totally different from that of John. Ezekiel was summoned to measure the temple for restoration. The temple had been destroyed by the Babylonians in 586 B.C., and the prophet believed that the exiles would return and rebuild the temple. This was accomplished when Zerubbabel and Joshua returned from Babylonian captivity.

Contrary to the command given to Ezekiel, John is told to measure the temple for destruction. If that event in the life of Jews is not so obvious in chapter 11, the destruction of Jerusalem becomes more evident later in the document. Is the author alluding to the destruction of the temple in 11:1-2? If so, the sanctuary and the people who worship in it are preserved. Yet this did not happen. The writer knew that the temple and the temple area were both destroyed by the Romans in A.D. 70. The outer court of the temple that was the area for the Gentiles to worship in was trampled under foot and destroyed by the Romans as well. Are these two verses to be interpreted allegorically? Some scholars[4] have suggested that this is what John has done. They base their conclusions on John's allegorizing the two witnesses. Consequently, the spiritual meaning would be a separation of the true Israel of God (disloyal Jews and dedicated Christians) from the false Israel of God (faithful Jews and apostate Christians). It is true that the author later makes a distinction between false Israel and true Israel, but if he has made a contrast here, it would have to be by anticipation because we have not been ushered into the Christian era.

What does John indicate by the 42 months and 1260 days? Also, what does he mean by the two witnesses? These and other numbers are found in Daniel. They appear in Revelation as the above and in other forms such as three and a half years, three and a half days, times, times, and half a time. All of these numbers represent a time of persecution in both Daniel and Revelation. But who are the two witnesses who are to prophesy for 1260 days, who are clothed in sackcloth and calling the people to repentance? The author does not call them by name, but he uses the prophet Zechariah to refer to Joshua, the high priest, and Zerubbabel, the spiritual leaders of the Jews after the return from Babylonian exile. There are also allusions to Moses and Elijah. In the Old Testament witnesses come in pairs. There are Moses and Aaron, Joshua and Caleb, Joshua and Zerubbabel, Elijah and Elisha. Jesus sent his disciples in pairs on a trial missionary journey. The mendicant members of the Essene community also went throughout Palestine in groups of two. It is also possible that John had in mind the Jewish law that required two or more witnesses to confirm their testimony in the law court. At any rate, John is telling us that the Jews in Jerusalem had ample opportunities to submit to God's sovereignty in the past by means of the oracles of the prophets calling the people to repentance.

We are reminded that Jesus said, "It is impossible for a prophet to be killed outside of Jerusalem" (Luke 13:33). He also said in his lament over Jerusalem, "Jerusalem, Jerusalem, the city that kills the prophets and stones those who are sent to it! How often I have desired to gather your children together as a hen gathers her brood under her wings, and you were not willing" (Matt 23:37 and Lucan parallel). Again Jesus reminded the Pharisees that they adorned the tombs of the prophets who were put to death because they did not conform to the *status quo*, yet these teachers would do the same as their fathers did if the prophets did not agree with them. Jesus went on to say, "Therefore I send you prophets, sages, scribes, some of whom you will kill and crucify, and some you will flog in your synagogues and pursue from town to town" (Matt 23:34).

All of those words of Jesus must have been in the background of John's thinking as he wrote. This is why he can, in a spiritual sense, equate Jerusalem with Sodom and Egypt. Somehow or another John ties in the beast, who ascends from the abyss, with the rejection of God's word in Jerusalem. The actual work of the beast, the incarnation of Satan, does not come under our purview until chapters 13 and 17. There could be a veiled allusion in 11:7-13 to the death of John the Baptist and Jesus whose messages were rejected by the religious leaders in Judea.

When the seventh angel blows his shofar, the great mystery of God (10:7) that was declared by the prophets is fulfilled. Loud voices from heaven announce, "The kingdom of the world has become the kingdom of our Lord and his Messiah, and he shall reign forever and ever." After this proclamation, the twenty-four elders fall on their faces and worship God with a hymn of praise. Immediately the heavenly temple is opened, and the Seer gets a glimpse of the ark of the covenant. The ark has been lost since the destruction of the temple by the Babylonians. We have now come into the Christian era.

To describe more fully the inauguration of the Christian movement, the Seer of Patmos sets up a scene in heaven. He does not say that he saw the event, but merely "there was seen" in the heaven above. A woman gave birth to a male child, and a red dragon attempted to devour the child upon delivery. Who is this woman? Various interpretations have been given. She represents Mary, the mother of Jesus, the inner Israel composed of loyal Jews and loyal Christians, the true Israel of God, or the primitive church. Since we have come into the Christian era, more than likely she represents those who have confessed faith in Christ—the true Israel of God. Who is the dragon? The word drakon in Greek is a serpent and not the medieval dragon with claws and flames of fires issuing from his mouth. The dragon is further identified as the devil, Satan, the ancient serpent (of the garden of Eden), and the deceiver of the world. He is the personification of all that is evil.

Michael, an archangel and the prince of Israel, with his angels defeated Satan and his angels in a war waged in heaven. Michael overcame Satan and his angels, and threw them down to the earth. In apocalyptic literature the defeat of the evil forces in heaven assured a victory over the evil forces on earth. When the male child (Christ) was born, he escaped the angry Satan and demonic forces by being caught up into heaven. The author seems to mean by this the resurrection of Christ. We are reminded of what Paul said in 1 Corinthians 2:7-8. There he discusses the wisdom of this age as over against the wisdom of God. If the rulers of this age (meaning demons and Satan) had understood the secret and hidden wisdom of God, they would not have crucified Christ because the crucifixion turned out to be a defeat for them. He implies here that Pilate and the Jewish leaders were prompted by the demonic powers to have Jesus put to death.

When Satan could not exterminate the true Israel of God (the primitive church), he sought to destroy the woman's offspring. By the use of "commandments of God" and "the testimony to Jesus," John includes the loyal Jews and the loyal Christians who were persecuted for their faith in God.

In keeping with the incarnation of God in Christ, John shows us that the dragon (Satan) becomes incarnate in the beast (the Roman emperor) to continue his persecution of the Christian movement. The beast is introduced in chapter 11, but now we get a clearer picture of who he is. He rises from the sea as in Daniel 7, yet John's beast combines the powers of the four empires in Daniel to show the extreme ruthlessness of the Roman empire. To the Roman emperor and the Roman empire the dragon gives his power to persecute the saints. John says that the number of the beast is 666. The number six is an imperfect number. Thus, the triplication of 6 represents consummate evil. Who is this beast with the number 666. It is generally agreed that it is Nero Caesar in cryptic form of Hebrew letters of the alphabet representing numbers as follows: Nun-50, Resh-200, Waw-6, Nun-50, Qoph-100, Samech-60, and Resh-200. The numbers add up to 666, and the name from the letters is Neron Kaisar. Some manuscripts give the number 616, which means that the final nun is omitted giving simply Nero Kaisar.

From the above calculations, we would assume that the writer has Nero Caesar in mind. Yet Nero Caesar did not persecute the Christians in the provinces, nor did he put to death those who did not worship him. In A.D. 64, he blamed the Christians in Rome for burning a slum section of the city when in realty he was the arsonist. Many Christians were put to death, but the persecution was limited to Rome. John inserts in chapter 13 "whose mortal wound was healed" to make it clear that it was not Nero but a Nero who was revived in Domitian. After the suicide or assassination of Nero in A.D. 68, a legend was circulated in the provinces saying that Nero still lived. Furthermore, in chapter 17 where the Seer lists the number of kings, he says that the beast who "was and is not, it is an eighth" (v. 11). Here also he meant Domitian. The order of the Roman emperors was Augustus, Tiberius, Caligula, Claudius, Nero, Vespasian, Titus, and Domitian.

In addition to the beast that arose from the sea representing the Roman emperor who was in the incarnation of Satan, another beast arose from the land. This beast represented those who implemented emperor worship in the provinces. In Acts the priests of the emperor cult were friends of Paul and begged him not to enter the theater lest some harm come to him (19:30). The situation was somewhat different under the reign of Domitian who demanded recognition of his divine character with far greater persistence than his predecessors. To refuse the proper worship of the emperor through his representative priests of the cult was an act of treason.

Domitian could not force the Jews to worship him as god because Judaism had a legal status in the Roman empire. Their immunity did not guarantee exemption from occasional severe treatment, however. Unless they would submit to the written and oral law, the Jews were not likely to stick their necks out for Christians. The Christians did not have a legal status in the empire, and they were "sitting ducks" for the full measure of Domitian's persecution.

When the early Christians proclaimed the gospel in the Hellenistic world, they encountered an immense variety of religious beliefs. Consequently, Christianity could establish itself without incurring a risk other than suspicion and prejudice. The situation was far different when an emperor wished to force the people to worship him as god. The emperor represented all the greatness and majesty of the Roman world. His power had united the vast communities of races, nations, and languages from the Persian Gulf to the Atlantic Ocean and from the cataracts of the Nile to the Scottish border into one body politic of peace. The emperor was the symbol of all that expressed law and order, civilization, arts, learning, commerce, and trade.

In 45 B.C., a statue was erected to Julius Caesar in Rome that bore the inscription "the invincible God". After his assassination in 44 B.C., the title *divus* (deity) was given to him, and he was enrolled among the powers of heaven. Augustus refused the title *divus*, but in 27 B.C., he was called Augustus instead of Octavian. Nevertheless, the word Augustus has the significance of one worshiped. Thus the imperial cult was established, and in this cultus the Christians could not participate. They must be loyal to the Lord Jesus Christ and disown loyalty to Domitian as Lord.

There was a similarity between Roman emperor worship and Christianity. Both attempted to promote a universal religion. Both believed in the incarnation of deity in human form. They were recent religions, and they had to compete with regional religions and also with each other. In both full allegiance was required. In Christianity it was loyalty to Jesus Christ as Lord, and in the emperor cult it was loyalty to Caesar as Lord. In a face-to-face encounter the Christians who were less powerful bore the stigma of treason and endured pain and suffering to the point of death.

In the forefront of the backdrop of the beast, his priests, and his army of worshipers, John presents us with the scene of 144,000. They stand on Mount Zion (not the earthly one in Jerusalem but the heavenly Zion) with the Lamb. They have the Lamb's name and the Father's name written on their foreheads in contrast to the mark of the beast. Who are the 144,000? In chapter 6 we observed that 144,000 from the tribes of Israel were sealed for protection. Is this the same group? John says they are the ones who have not defiled themselves with women. They are virgins. Are we to take this literally and understand that these are celibates? Virgin is to be taken symbolically. The author does not indicate that these are men who had no intercourse with women. He has in mind the sexual rites connected with pagan temples that Gentile Christians found it difficult to renounce.

The 144,000 (the number is not to be taken literally) denote those who refused to participate in pagan practices and remained firm in their dedication to Christ. Again John comes back to the *Tamid* ritual with *to arnion hestos* (the lamb having taken a stand and is still standing) indicating that Christ was the Lamb for the daily sacrifice. Also, the new song that is sung by the 144,000 before the throne, the four living creatures, and the elders has its place in the daily sacrifice because each day of the week the Levites sang a new psalm for the ceremony.

The interlude of chapter 14 continues with John's vision of three angels flying in midheaven. Each angel carries a message that is reminiscent of the apocalyptic discourse in Mark 13. The first angel's message has a kinship with Mark 13:30. The second angel proclaims the destruction of Babylon, which is Jerusalem. This reminds us of the statement of Jesus relative to the temple: "Not one stone will be left here upon another" (v. 2). The third angel proclaims doom on those who worship the beast. This message reminds us of the warnings of false messiahs and false prophets who will arise and lead people astray (v. 22).

These three visions are followed by the Seer beholding the son of man (Christ) coming on a cloud with a sickle in his hand to reap the grain harvest. The grain harvest designates the gathering of the elect so that they would not have to endure the bloody catastrophe of the fall of Jerusalem. The faithful Christians and the loyal Jews would be spared the suffering connected with the destruction of Jerusalem. Another angel appears with a sharp sickle to harvest the grapes. The grapes are put into a wine press that was the wine press of the wrath of God. This harvest is the degenerate Jews who were destroyed with the fall of Jerusalem.

The Seven Bowls of Wrath

John saw another sign in heaven great and wonderful. The seven angels came out of the heavenly temple with bowls of God's wrath to pour upon the earth. In the *Tamid* ritual this is the time for the pouring of the wine offering at the base of the altar. The pouring in this ritual was for reconciliation. But, unlike the *Tamid*, the pouring out of God's wrath is for destruction.

The first four angels who empty their bowls give a repetition of judgments already encountered with the sounding of the first four shofars. The crises come in the form of catastrophic forces in nature and recall the plagues in Egypt. The fifth, sixth, and seventh bowls of wrath describe the situation in the Roman empire prior to and including the destruction of Jerusalem. The fifth depicts the civil war in Rome after Nero committed suicide in A.D. 68. It was indeed a time of darkness. Vitellius, Galba, and Otho contended with each other over the right to be Nero's successor. When the sixth bowl is poured out, Vespasian is established as emperor. Titus, the son of Vespasian, had withdrawn the Roman legions from Palestine where the Romans had fought the Jewish insurrectionists since A.D. 66. He went to Alexandria, Egypt, not only to regroup his forces for the final assault against Jerusalem, but also to be closer to Rome and lend his support to Vespasian in his claim to be the successor to Nero.

After Vespasian was crowned emperor, Titus moved into Palestine with his legions and assembled at Armageddon. This is reminiscent of the time Josiah, the king of Judah, was defeated by Pharaoh Necho and the Egyptians. In 609 B.C., Josiah tried to block the Egyptians from going through the valley of Megiddo to support the Assyrians in their war against the Babylonians. Armageddon, which means the mountain of armageddon, is inaccurate. Megiddo was a valley. Apparently what the Seer meant by this was Mount Zion-Jerusalem. Those who are worried about the battle of Armageddon, worry no more! The battle has already been fought with the sacking of the city Jerusalem.

When the last angel empties his bowl of wrath, the city of Jerusalem is split into three rival factions: the Zealot forces of Simon ben Giora, John of Gischala, and Eleazer ben Shimeon. While these dissenting parties are fighting each other in the city, the Romans are bombarding the city from without with tremendous stones. The great city Babylon, the harlot city represented by Jerusalem, is destroyed. Official Judaism, which according to John is the false Israel of God, becomes a burnt offering of the Tamid ritual, and its smoke goes up forever and ever.

Most New Testament scholars believe that the harlot city Babylon is a reference to Rome. There is nothing in the scene to indicate Rome, but there is compelling evidence to support Jerusalem. (1) With the exception of the seven cities mentioned at the beginning of the document, there is no other city alluded to in the book other than Jerusalem. (2) The destruction of Jerusalem is the center of concern in the apocalyptic discourse in Mark 13. (3) Jerusalem had persecuted the prophets and Christians. (4) In chapter 11, John calls Jerusalem by the name of Sodom where Christ was crucified. (5) The prophets in the Old Testament called Jerusalem or Judah a harlot. The historical Isaiah said that the faithful city (Jerusalem) became a harlot (1:21). Jeremiah criticized Judah for playing the part of a harlot (3:6). The prophet Ezekiel who was a primary source for the author of Revelation gave a lengthy discussion of the harlotry of Jerusalem (chaps. 16, 23). (6) Ezekiel's lamentation over Tyre (27:1–28:19) and Isaiah's oracle against Babylon (21:1-10) seem to have been used by the Seer in his description of Jerusalem.

In the Sibylline Oracles and perhaps in 1 Peter, Babylon is a cryptic name for Rome, but beyond these two documents we have no identification of Rome with Babylon. Josephus,[5] the Jewish historian, was an eyewitness to the destruction of Jerusalem and recorded some apocalyptic elements prior to the fall of the city that are closely akin to those of the book of Revelation. Josephus is in accord with John when he says, "It is God, therefore, it is God who is with the Romans, and is bringing upon it (Jerusalem) the fire of purification, and is rooting up the city which is full of pollution."

Chapter 18 is filled with lamentations of various groups of people who regretted the fall of Jerusalem. We hear the cries of the merchants who had traded their goods with the city. No longer could they sell their gold, silver, jewels, pearls, fine linen, purple, silk, ivory, iron, marble, spies, perfumes, wine, horses and chariots, and slaves. The kings of the earth wept when they saw the city burning. The shipmasters and sailors who stood afar lamented over the sack of Jerusalem and cried out, "What city was like the great city" (v. 18).

Contrary to the sadness expressed by those who had profited by Jerusalem, we observe that there is joy, exultation, and glee manifested by a great multitude in heaven. With a loud voice they cry out,

> Hallelujah! Salvation and glory and power to our God, for his judgments are true and just; he has judged the great whore who corrupted the earth with her fornication, and he has avenged on her the blood of his servants. (19:1-2)

When the author of Revelation wrote his document, he was aware that Jerusalem had fallen. To him the city represented a reaction to the Christian movement. Jesus, through the malicious intrigues of the Jewish religious leaders, was crucified. Stephen, the first Christian martyr, was stoned to death in the city. James, the son of Zebedee, and

James, the brother of Jesus, also suffered martyrdom. There were many others who endured suffering from the hands of the religious leaders. Undoubtedly, the author of Revelation was delighted with the destruction of the city. Throughout his book he separates the faithful Jews from the disloyal Jews. The degenerate Jews were the false Israel of God, and the genuine Christians and Jews were the true Israel of God.

Now that the false Israel has been liquidated, it is time for the revelation of the true Israel. John hears an angel say, "Blessed are those who are invited to the marriage supper of the Lamb" (19:9). He sees Christ on a white horse, coming to claim his bride, the Church.

What about the other enemy of the author of Revelation? This is the Roman emperor who set himself up as God. What happens to him and all those who pay homage to him? In a few verses John shows that this evil force will be annihilated as well. The beast (Domitian) and the false prophet of the beast (priests of the emperor cult) are thrown into Gehenna, the lake of fire that burns with sulfur. The army of the beast is slain, and their bodies are eaten by the vultures. John knows that this victory has not been achieved in his time, but he looks for the judgment of Christ to destroy this enemy.

In light of the introduction to Revelation and the concluding verses in chapter 22, we might suppose that John is finished with his witness to what is to occur soon and that the time is near (1:1, 3; 22:7, 10, 12, 20). With victory on the threshold, what else is there to consider? Like Ezekiel and Jewish apocalyptists, he feels compelled to deal with the end time. For him it is "not over until it was over."

Though the Seer of Patmos sees through the eyes of faith that the present threat to Christianity by Domitian is terminated, he knows that Satan is still alive and "kicking." Therefore, he has a vision of an angel who binds Satan and throws him into the abyss. There he will remain for 1,000 years. John is dependent on apocalyptic literature in this scene of the binding of Satan. In 1 Enoch 10:4, the Lord says to Raphael, one of the archangels, "Bind Azazel by his hands and feet and throw him into the darkness." In Jubilees 48:15, Mastema is bound by chains so that he cannot harass the Israelites.

117

There is a temporary lull in the evil activity of Satan, but when he is released, he will return filled with fury, rage, and unrestrained anger to continue his dirty work. During the same period of time, the loyal Jews and loyal Christians who had their heads chopped off because they were obedient to God will be raised from the dead and reign with Christ. Is the reign in heaven or on earth? The author does not say. He adopts the view of other Jewish apocalyptists that those who were martyrs for God had the edge over the ordinary believers and should receive a greater reward. John uses the word for beheading. The Greek verb is *pelekizein*, which is from the substantive *pelekus*, which means axe. In other words, they were the ones who had been axed.

If we accept the author at his face value, the only ones who will participate in this reign of Christ are the martyrs, and the 1,000-years reign bears no meaning to those who do not undergo this ordeal. In 2 Enoch the last stage of world history will last for 1,000 years. Another apocalyptic work envisions God's messiah as reigning for 400 years. After that the end time will come (Apocalypse of Ezra 7:28-44). The apocalyptists vary in their understanding of the glorious age to come. Some hold to a permanent kingdom on earth, others to a temporary rule of peace and prosperity on earth and a permanent golden age in heaven, and still others omit the permanent or temporary rule on earth and confine it to heaven. John does not commit himself to earth or heaven in his reasoning, but merely tells us that it will be a temporary reign.

The Seer of Patmos was under no illusion relative to the evil activity of Satan as soon as he was released from prison. The devil gets ready for his final fling of deception by summoning the nations from the four corners of the earth. The nations are led by Gog and Magog. Here again the Seer takes a scene from the prophet Ezekiel; however, in Ezekiel it is Gog from the land of Magog. The author of the Sibylline Oracles is guilty of the same mistake as Revelation (III, 319f.) by individualizing Magog rather than considering it a nation. Who is this Gog from the land of Magog? Josephus identifies the Magogites as Scythians (Antiquities of the Jews, I.6.1). One of the recurring themes in Jeremiah is the threat of an invasion of the people from the north

(1:13, 14; 5:15-17; 6:1-5). Jeremiah alludes to the Scythians, a tribe of marauders who lived north of the Black Sea and in later times were known as the Cossacks. Though they made raids in various parts of the Mideast, they did not invade Judah. Jeremiah is mistaken in his prediction, but Ezekiel follows up on this and gives the name Gog to the leader of the invading force.

Chapters 38–39 of Ezekiel are very odd. In chapter 37, Ezekiel has a vision of the reunification of the tribes of Israel under a descendant of David. He sees Israel as a valley of dry bones that will be revitalized. It is his prediction of the return of the exiles. God will make a covenant of peace with the exiles that return, and he will bless them. But with this vision of a time of peace and prosperity for Israel, we are suddenly hit with another foe in chapter 38. It is the mystical Gog of the land of Magog.

Some scholars maintain that chapters 38–39 were written by someone other than Ezekiel because of the loose connection between chapters 37 and 40, and also because of the more mystical elements contained in them. This section of Ezekiel attempts a reinterpretation of Jeremiah's prophecy of an enemy from the north. For the apocalyptist who composed these two chapters, the danger now becomes a battle with a mythical king and his army that ushers in the end time and heralds the coming of God's kingdom.

The Seer of Patmos in using Ezekiel as one of his sources sees that there must be a final engagement between the forces of evil and the powers of good. Gog and his army "surrounded the camp of the saints and the beloved city" (v. 9). The "beloved city" is not the earthly Jerusalem because it has been destroyed. This city is symbolic of the church, the new Israel of God. The enemy was consumed by fire that descended from heaven, and Satan, the instigator of the plot to blot out Christianity, was thrown into Gehenna. Thus, the present age comes to an end, and the final judgment is about to begin.

A similar picture of a terminal fight between good and evil is found in other apocalyptic writings. Though the authors of these works fail to mention Gog of the land of Magog or Gog and Magog, it is clear that they reinterpret the Ezekiel passages to which we have referred. In the Apocalypse of Ezra we see "an innumerable company of men" who "are gathered together from the four winds of heaven" to engage the Messiah in battle, and by supernatural means the Messiah destroys them (13:5, 33f.). Again, in the Apocalypse of Baruch we are presented with a final fling of evil, and the Messiah summons the nations to appear before him. Some are spared, and some are destroyed (70:7-10).

In John's vision of the final judgment, he sees God seated on a great white throne ready to render a verdict. On two occasions the apostle Paul said that God dispensed the final act of judgment (Rom 2:16; 14:10). In two instances he declared that Christ would be the judge (2 Cor 5:10; Acts 17:31). In John's scene of the final judgment the Lamb and his saints are unnoted. The twenty-four elders, the multitude of angels, and the four living creatures are absent. God alone makes the judgment. How do the martyrs who reigned with Christ for 1,000 years figure in this scene? Apparently, John considers the martyrs, who were raised in the first resurrection, as those who are exempt from the final judgment.

There is a general resurrection, and the decision as to the destiny of individuals is based on "books" and "the book of Life." One set of books records every person's deeds, and the other book is a register of the elect. Does the Seer mean that "the books" in which are kept the deeds of people can have an influence on their destiny? Can persons who do works of righteousness be delivered and escape doom? Can they also by their good deeds be listed in the other book, the book of Life? Does the author take into consideration here, as he does elsewhere in the document, the faithful Jews who were obedient to the commandments of God?

The apostle Paul who constantly contended that people come into a right relationship with God by faith in Jesus Christ apart from the works of the Law said, "For all of us must appear before the judgment seat of Christ, so that each may receive recompense for what has been done in the body, whether good or evil" (2 Cor 5:10). Again, in Romans 2:5-7, Paul said, "But by your hard and impenitent heart you are storing up wrath for yourself on the day of wrath when God's righteous judgment will be revealed. For he will repay according to each one's deeds." Note, in this passage Paul is speaking to an imaginary Jew. It is conceivable that the opening up of the book of life is not a matter of securing deliverance for those whose names are inscribed in it, but rather an attempt to justify the judgment of God on the sinners who reject God. At any rate, those not included in the book of life are thrown into Gehenna with Satan and all his cohorts.

The New Jerusalem

Pursuant to the final judgment, it remains for the author to tell us of the future happiness and bliss of the righteous and faithful. He does this with another vision. Based upon the prediction of the Isaiah of the Restoration (65:17; 66:22) and the reinterpretations of Isaiah by the Jewish apocalyptists, John sees a new heaven and a new earth. The apocalyptic writers believed that God's creation had been usurped by Satan and his legions, and as a result was under the power of wickedness. The usurped creation will be restored, the corrupted universe will be cleansed, and the created world will be re-created. The end time was to be as the beginning of time. In the Epistle of Barnabas, a Christian apocalyptic document of the second century A.D., the author states on divine authority, "I will make the last things as the first" (6:13).

John also sees the New Jerusalem coming down from God out of heaven. The New Jerusalem is symbolic of the new residence of the true Israel of God. We have previously noted in the examination of Jewish apocalyptic literature that the writers believed there was a heavenly Jerusalem that was a counterpart of the Jerusalem on earth. They also conflated the heavenly Jerusalem with a return to the garden of Eden where Adam and Eve got their start. John also conflates the two. After he gives a glowing picture of the New Jerusalem in chapter 21, he brings us back to the garden of Eden in chapter 22.

The Seer of Patmos is a bit incoherent and inconsistent in 22:15. He has told us that all the wicked and evil ones were thrown into

Gehenna at the final judgment, but now he says that outside the gate of the New Jerusalem and the garden of Eden are dogs, sorcerers, fornicators, murderers, idolaters, and every one who loves and practices a lie. If all of these were supposed to have been destroyed, where do they come from? We are left to our imagination by the author.

The main thrust of the message of John can be summarized in a few words. He was firmly convinced that nothing could stop the spread of Christianity. Neither false Judaism nor emperor persecution could prevail against the revelation of God in Jesus Christ. This hopeful theme runs throughout the book. The vast majority of his material gives scenes of the past. Some are in the present, but very little has to do with the future. He had an unwavering faith in Christ's impending judgment on Domitian, the Roman emperor. In reality, his document should have ended with chapter 19 and the sayings of Christ's immediate coming in chapter 22. Yet he must have thought that he ought to give an addendum to the book, and to do this he incorporated ideas advanced in Jewish apocalyptic literature that were reinterpretations of the Old Testament prophets.

Notes

[1] Justin Martyr, *Dialogue with Trypho*, 81.

[2] Philip Carrington, *The Meaning of Revelation* (London: S.P.C.K., 1931).

[3] Moses Maimonides, *Guide for the Perplexed*, 3:45.

[4] Philip Carrington, *The Meaning of the Revelation* (London, S.P.C.K., 1931) 181-91; and William Milligan, *The Book of Revelation* (London: Hodder & Stoughton, 1909) 169-84.

[5] Flavius Josephus, *Wars of the Jews*, VI.5.

Conclusion

THE FUTURE WAS THEN

In our study of apocalyptic literature we have discovered that the writers held many teachings in common. The authors had a pessimistic concept of history. There was no hope that people could make a change in society by being obedient to the demands of God. The wickedness and sinfulness of humanity would continue to increase to the point that the world would be saturated with evil. It would take a catastrophic intervention by God to cleanse the earth of unrighteousness. Their optimism was centered in God's action in history because they believed they were powerless against Satan and his supernatural cohorts.

All of the apocalyptists had a deep concern for the justice of God. How can God allow such suffering and pain to be inflicted on the righteous by the unrighteous? When will God avenge the martyrs? Why does God permit the injustices to go unnoticed in life? Why does God let evil prevail over humanity? These and many other questions were asked because the writers believed God was just. In spite of their anxiety concerning the justice of God, they had an impassioned conviction of the righteous rule of God and a bold assurance of a moral government in the world.

When the doctrine of the resurrection from the dead emerged in Judaism, the apocalyptists were the originators, developers, and propagators of it. This teaching was accepted by the Pharisees and became a strong belief in normative Judaism. The doctrine was passed on to Christianity, but not just in the form of a theory and hope. It became a reality in the resurrection of Jesus Christ. It was this hope in a hereafter that gave them the assurance that if no justice existed in this life, a rectification would manifest itself in the age to come.

The apocalyptists were firm believers in determinism, a tenet foreign to the teaching of the prophets. They looked upon history as the working out of a predestined plan of God, and nothing could change that fixed blueprint. Their preoccupation was with the end of the age. According to their calculations, the end of the age would occur in their own time. They offered revelations of the last days of the present epoch of history, the final judgment, and the golden age to follow. Their visions were constructed with fantastic minuteness using mind-boggling and bizarre imagery.

What is the relevance of the apocalyptic thought in our day? For those who have studied Jewish and Christian apocalyptic literature and waded through its symbolism, there is nothing but praise and admiration for their attempts to cope with the problem of evil and the justice of God. For those who are acquainted only with Daniel and Revelation, these books become a draft for the predictions of the termination of the age. Little do they realize that these and other such works were written as tracts for the times. The writers did not have future generations in mind when they wrote. Their great concern was about persecution in their own day, and they looked forward to the time when God would break into human history and relieve them of oppression.

It might be a surprise to some that the early Christians accepted Jewish apocalyptic writings and reworked them. The only difference between Jewish and Christian writings of this sort is that Jesus Christ is placed at the center of all that is given. Just as the Jewish visionaries adapted and readapted the oracles of the Old Testament prophets and each other, so Christians adapted and reworked the Jewish writings for their own needs. If the Christians had not preserved these documents, they probably would be lost forever. If they had been lost, it is doubtful we could have ever understood this genre of literature or comprehended the meaning of apocalyptic elements in the Old and New Testaments.

If Daniel, an apocalyptic work, was admitted to the Hebrew canon of the Old Testament, and if Revelation, an apocalyptic document, was finally accepted into the canon of the New Testament, what is to prevent us from canonizing the many Jewish apocalyptic writings as well as other Christian documents of the same kind? Since Jude, 2 Peter, Hebrews, Paul, and the author of Revelation made frequent use of them, does not their usage indicate some degree of validity? We know that the Shepherd of Hermas, the Apocalypse of Peter, and the Epistle of Barnabas were all acclaimed as scripture in certain Christian circles.

It is disturbing that some ministers today take the books of Daniel and Revelation and treat them as prophetic books when in reality they are apocalyptic documents. Ministers spend time and energy trying to figure out the termination of the age. When they think the plan of God is fully deciphered, they preach sermons fooling the congregation into believing they know the end is near.

Years ago I was present in a discussion group led by one of my former professors. The discussion centered around the book of Revelation. A prominent pastor was present. He said that he had been preaching a series of sermons on the Second Coming and the termination of all things. My professor asked, "Do you believe the things that you are telling your people?" He immediately replied, "Not completely, but the people like what I say, and I am interested in pleasing the people." Too often this is true. An attempt is made to please the congregation, rather than tell them what they ought to know. As someone has said, "You are more popular if you entertain the goats rather than feed the sheep."

It has been nearly 2,100 years since the first Jewish apocalyptists predicted the end of the age, and they anticipated this event to happen in their lifetime. In fact, 1,900 years ago, the Seer of Patmos expected the occurrence to be soon. About 59 years previous to the Seer, the apostle Paul believed that the termination of the age was near, and he expected it to take place while he was alive. Time has shown they were all mistaken. The future they contemplated was then. More years have intervened from the beginning of apocalypticism until our day than have intervened from the time of Abraham to the rise of this sort of literature. This should tell us something about modern-day predictions. Perhaps we should safeguard ourselves with a reverent silence about subject matter on which our predecessors felt cocksure. Those who get the apocalyptic fever and cannot endure the tension between the this-worldly and the otherworldly long for the consummation of history. The odds are perhaps a billion to one that they will die before this happens. Therefore, it is incumbent upon us to live the Christian life and leave the rest to God.

Bibliography

Ashcraft, Morris. *Revelation.* Vol. 12, *The Broadman Bible Commentary.* Nashville: Broadman Press, 1972.

Bloch, Joshua. *On the Apocalyptic in Judaism.* Monograph Series, no. 11, *The Jewish Quarterly Review.* Philadelphia: The Dropsie College for Hebrew and Cognate Learning, 1952.

Brandon, S. C. F. *The Fall of Jerusalem and the Christian Church.* 2d ed. London: S.P.C.K., 1957.

Burkitt, F. C. *Jewish and Christian Apocalypses.* London: The British Academy, 1913.

Carrington, Philip. *The Meaning of Revelation.* London: S.P.C.K., 1931.

Carpenter, J. Estlin. *The Johannine Writings.* London: Constable & Co., 1927.

Charles, R. H., ed. *The Apocrypha and Pseudepigrapha of the Old Testament.* 2 vols. Oxford: University Press, reissued in 1963.

——————. *Eschatology.* New York: Schocken Press, 1963.

Frost, Stanley B. *The Old Testament Apocalyptic.* London: Epworth Press, 1952.

Lohse, Eduard. *The New Testament Environment.* Nashville: Abingdon Press, 1974.

Milligan, William. *The Book of Revelation.* London: Hodder & Stoughton, 1909.

Newman, Barclay M., Jr. *Rediscovering the Book of Revelation.* Valley Forge PA: Judson Press, 1968.

Rowley, H. H. *The Relevance of Apocalyptic.* London: Lutterworth Press, 1947.

Russell, D. S. *The Method and Message of Jewish Apocalyptic.* Philadelphia: Westminster Press, 1984.

Shanks, Hershel, James C. Vanderkam, P. Kyle McCarter, and James A. Sanders. *The Dead Sea Scrolls After Forty Years.* Washington DC: Biblical Archeology Society, 1991.

Snaith, Norman. *The Jews from Cyrus to Herod.* Surrey: Religious Education Press, 1949.

Sparks, H. F. D., ed. *The Apocryphal Old Testament.* Oxford: Clarendon Press, 1984.